### E. Franklin Frazier on the Negro Press:

"The Negro press is not only one of the most successful business enterprises owned and controlled by Negroes; it is the chief medium of communication which creates and perpetuates the world of make-believe for the black bourgeoisie. Although the Negro press declares itself to be the spokesman for the Negro group as a whole, it represents essentially the interests and outlook of the black bourgeoisie. Its demand for equality for the Negro in American life is concerned primarily with opportunities which will benefit the black bourgeoisie economically and enhance the social status of the Negro. The Negro press reveals the inferiority complex of the black bourgeoisie and provides a documentation of the attempts of this class to seek compensations for its hurt self-esteem and exclusion from American life. Its exaggerations concerning the economic well-being and cultural achievements of Negroes, its emphasis upon Negro 'society' all tend to create a world of make-believe into which the black bourgeoisie can escape from its inferiority and inconsequence in American society."

# E. FRANKLIN FRAZIER

# BLACK

# BOURGEOISIE

**The Rise of a New Middle
Class in the United States**

With a New Preface
by the Author

**COLLIER BOOKS**

NEW YORK, N.Y.

102804

# Contents

## Part II—The World of Make-Believe

# Preface

THIS BOOK FIRST appeared in France as one of the studies in the collection known as *Recherches en Sciences Humaines*.[1] When the French edition was published I expected that like so many social science studies it would become lost on the shelves of university libraries. It came as a pleasant surprise, therefore, to learn that it attracted sufficient attention in the academic world for it to be made the basis of the MacIver Lectureship award by the American Sociological Society in 1956. When the English edition was published in the United States in 1957, I was even more surprised by the controversy which it aroused among Negroes and by the unfavorable reactions of many whites.

The reaction of the Negro community is understandable when one realizes the extent to which the book created the shock of self-revelation. In fact, if one should undertake to conceptualize the reaction of the Negro community, the initial reaction—at least on the part of its more articulate leaders—was one of shock. It appeared that middle class Negroes were able to see themselves for the first time and, as they feared, in the way they appeared to outsiders. They did not challenge the truth of the picture which had been presented so much as they were shocked that a Negro would dare place on display their behavior and innermost thoughts. Their naive attitude towards their behavior and outlook on life was strikingly revealed in the remark of a journalist whose publication had been drawn on for much illustrative material in the book. When I met his criticism of quoting materials by asking him if his publication was not a reliable source of information, he replied that the facts in the book looked and sounded different from what they did where they appeared in his magazine.

Following the initial shock of self-revelation was intense

[1] *Bourgeoisie Noire*. Paris: Librairie Plon, 1955.

anger on the part of many leaders in the Negro community. This anger was based largely upon their feeling that I had betrayed Negroes by revealing their life to the white world. I was attacked by some Negroes as being bitter because I had not been accepted socially and by others as having been paid to defame the Negro. In one Negro newspaper there was a sly suggestion that Negroes should use violence to punish me for being a traitor to the Negro race. Some of the anger was undoubtedly due to the fact that I had revealed the real economic position of the Negro. They were particularly incensed by a mere statement of fact that the total assets of all Negro banks in the United States were less than those of a single small white bank in a small town in the State of New York.

The anger of the middle class over this statement showed how much they regarded the book as a threat to their economic interests. They had helped to create the myth of the vast purchasing power of Negroes which had become the justification for large corporations to employ Negro salesmen so as to exploit the Negro market.

It is interesting to note, however, that the anger on the part of the Negro community was not shared by all strata. From rumors and from what had appeared in book reviews in both white and Negro newspapers, some working class Negroes got the impression that I had written a book attacking "upper-class, light-skinned" Negroes. As a consequence I was even stopped on the street by working-class Negroes who shook my hand for having performed this long overdue service.

As the book became more widely read and discussed Negroes began to judge the book more soberly and in many cases not only to applaud my "courage" in writing the book but to say that it was an important contribution to an understanding of the Negro's plight in the United States. Numerous letters were sent directly to me and sometimes to the Negro newspapers defending the book or congratulating me on my courage. One minister wrote that the book should be read by every Negro preacher in the United States. Letters of this type continue to come to me and I am constantly invited to speak to forums and groups on the position and outlook of the new Negro middle class. This reaction of the Negro community presented a sharp contrast to what happened when the reaction of Negroes was characterized by anger. For example, I was invited by a Negro sorority to discuss the book but so much bitterness was aroused by the invitation that it had to be canceled. One leading member of the sorority accused me of having set the Negro race back fifty years. But such reactions are rare today and I am much more likely to receive copies of articles or speeches in which there are favorable references to the book, discussions of the book's implications or even documentation in support of its analysis.

The reaction of the white people outside the United States was different, on the whole, from that of white Americans. European and Latin American scholars praised the book, on the whole, as a contribution to social science and as a lucid analysis of what is happening to the American Negro. A liberal European scholar living in South Africa said that when she read the book her first reaction was, "My God, the American Negro has finally come of age; he is capable of self-analysis and self-criticism." Under the title, "Un Livre Explosif," a leading French newspaper, Le Monde (February 13, 1957) carried a perceptive summary review of the book. In fact, it was often European scholars who were most puzzled by the reactions of white Americans. A European told me two years ago that he could understand why middle-class Negroes might be angry about the book but that he could not understand the anger which it aroused among some white Americans. Let us turn to the reactions of some white Americans and undertake to explain them.

The critical reviews which appeared in American scholarly journals were concerned for the most part with questions involving methodology and the validity of my conclusions. In some of the more serious journals of opinion there also appeared critical reviews. But even in some of the scholarly reviews as well as in the serious journals of opinion there was either an implicit or explicit criticism that the book exhibited anger or lack of sympathy in its stark objectivity. A leading political analyst said that the book was cruel because if Negroes were happy in their world of make-believe, why should I feel it was my duty to let them know the truth about their real position in the United States? Although it appeared that many whites shared this opinion, there were others who welcomed the book as an explanation of the behavior of middle-class Negroes—behavior which had long puzzled them. Some of them came to me and stated frankly that they had been puzzled, for example, by the conspicuous consumption on the part of middle-class Negroes but that after reading the book they could understand it.

Perhaps the main reason for the bitter reaction on the part of some white Americans (some book stores refused to carry the book because it was "controversial") was that it destroyed or tended to destroy the image of Negroes which they wanted to present to the world at this time. The picture which white Americans wanted to present to the world was that although Negroes had been enslaved and had suffered many disabilities since Emancipation, on the whole they were well off economically, had gained civil rights, and had improved their social status. Therefore, what had happened to them during slavery, which was after all a mild paternalistic system, should be forgotten along with the other injustices which they have suffered since. Moreover, their economic position was superior to that of other peoples of the world, especially the colored peoples. One article published by a distinguished statesman even went so far as to state that Negroes were spending annually an amount equal to the annual national income of Canada.

Now, *Black Bourgeoisie* was a refutation of this image. It showed that slavery was a cruel and barbaric system that annihilated the Negro as a person, a fact which has been well-documented and substantiated in a recent book.[2] Moreover, the book also showed how, since Emancipation, Negroes

---

[2] Stanley M. Elkins, *Slavery, a Problem in American Institutional and Intellectual Life*. Chicago: The University of Chicago Press, 1959.

had been outsiders in American society. Finally, it demonstrated on the basis of factual knowledge that Negroes were not only at the bottom of the economic ladder but that all the pretended economic gains which Negroes were supposed to have made had not changed fundamentally their relative economic position in American life. It revealed also that the new Negro middle class was comprised almost entirely of wage earners and salaried professionals and that so-called Negro business enterprises amounted to practically nothing in the American economy. This was not, of course, the image of Negroes that white Americans wanted to present to the world, especially at a time when they were endeavoring to win the confidence and friendship of the colored world.

Very often the question is asked whether there is need for a revision of this book. Has not the economic position of the Negro middle classes changed? Have not middle-class Negroes become accustomed to their new prosperity and given up much of their conspicuous consumption? From the latest figures on the occupations and the incomes of middle-class Negroes there is no reason to revise what was written about the relative size of the middle class and their occupational status nor the source and amount of their incomes. The essential fact is that they still do not own any of the real wealth of America or play an important role in American business. And it is difficult to see how their economic position could change fundamentally within five years. In reply to the second question one would only need to read Negro newspapers and magazines to see to what extent conspicuous consumption is still the dominant pattern of this class. In the cities of the country middle-class Negro communities are expanding but they are characterized by the same conspicuous consumption the book describes. School teachers and college professors who earn less than $10,000 a year are building homes that cost $40,000 and $50,000 and entertaining lavishly. In this connection one is reminded of the article which appeared recently in a white publication on the Negro aristocracy and Negro millionaires.[3] It should

[3] Bill Davidson, "Our Negro Aristocracy," *The Saturday Evening Post*, January 13, 1962.

be noted that many Negroes resented this article as a mis-representation of the real economic position of Negro pro-fessional men and women. Since this article appeared I have received numerous letters and comments saying the article confirmed what I had said about the world of make-believe in which middle-class Negroes live.

There is, however, an important aspect of the development of the new Negro middle class that might have been included in this book and certainly could not be omitted from a more detailed study. It is strange that the omission was overlooked by American critics but suggested in a for-eign review. I am referring to the most recent accessions to the Negro middle classes who are prominent in the sit-ins and in the other protest movements against racial segregation. They do not have the same social background as the black bourgeoisie in my study who represent a fusion of the peas-ant and the gentleman. Although they have been influenced to some extent by the genteel tradition, on the whole, their social background is essentially that of the Negro folk. Very seldom can they or their parents claim ancestors among the mixed-blood aristocracy which was free before the Civil War.

Some attention must be given to two more serious criti-cisms of the book as it now stands. The first concerns the materials upon which the analyses are based. Here I am not concerned with the question of adequate samplings of middle-class Negroes with respect to attributes that can be treated statistically. I am referring especially to the analyses of the patterns of behavior and values of this class. Let me begin by stating that it would be difficult to secure a more reliable validation of this study in regard to patterns of behavior and style of life and values of the Negro middle class than that which has been provided in the letters and comments which have come to me from cities all over the country. These letters have stated first that they did not know that I had carried on researches in their community until they had read the book which provided such an authentic picture of the middle class in their city. In many cases they com-plained that the picture was so true to life that they could recognize the people by their behavior and verbal statements and their relation to the rest of the community. As a matter of fact, in most cases I had never made a study in their community. An amusing incident connected with this aspect of the study happened in one city where my junior colleagues had made a housing survey. After the English edition appeared, they were accused of having spied on the behavior of the middle classes and were threatened with a thrashing if they ever returned to that city. The majority of the materials upon which this study was based were materials on thousands of Negro families and many Negro communities which I had collected during studies over the years. For the purposes of this study, additional materials were collected from newspapers and magazines and from students from middle-class families. In many cases, as a participant-observer, I collected case materials in the same manner as an anthropologist gathers materials for studies.

Another criticism which deserves attention was that this study did not reveal anything peculiar to Negroes. This was a criticism offered not only by Negroes who are sensitive about being different from other people, but by white people as well. Some of them were the so-called liberal whites who, when any statement is made which might be considered derogatory concerning Negroes, are quick to say that the "same thing is found among whites." Other whites pointed out what is undoubtedly true: that this book dealt with behavior which is characteristic of middle-class people—white, black or brown. Some of my Jewish friends, including some young sociologists, went so far as to say that the book was the best account that they had ever read concerning middle-class Jews. Here I might repeat what I stated in the book: that the behavior of middle-class Negroes was an American phenomenon and that in writing, I was constantly tempted to make comparisons with middle-class whites, but that the book was essentially a case study of the new Negro middle class. It was not my intention to make a comparative study. As a case study of middle-class Negroes, it does show the peculiar conditions under which a middle class emerged among the Negro minority and the peculiar social and cultural heritage of the Negro middle class which was responsible for its outlook on life.

In retrospect when I consider the reaction of the Negro community and the criticisms of both Negroes and whites of all intellectual levels, I am reminded of a review of the French edition which appeared on the front page of a French newspaper published in the United States.[4] The review concluded with the questions: Would this book arouse heated discussions in which each protagonist would hold stubbornly to his particular opinion? Would it contribute to modifying the mentality of this elite which is oblivious of its duties and responsibilities? A partial answer was given to these questions by some of the young leaders of the sit-ins who said they did not aspire to become the middle-class Negroes described in *Black Bourgeoisie*. Finally, in regard to the charge that the presentation was brutal or cruel, I will only quote the words of a Catholic sociological review concerning the book: "A sad truth is better than a merry lie."

E. FRANKLIN FRAZIER

Howard University
February, 1962

[4] *Le Travailleur*. Worcester, Massachusetts, April 12, 1956.

# Introduction

THE PRESENCE OF at least 19,000,000 persons of Negro ancestry[1] * among the people of the United States is the outcome of the expansion of Europe which began in the fifteenth century and became firmly established during the succeeding two centuries.[2] As the result of this expansion Europeans met and conquered many primitive peoples, laid the basis for European settlements, and established commercial relations with the old civilizations of Asia and Africa. European expansion in the Americas became especially important for the economic development of Europe, since the production of tobacco, sugar, and cotton, which were exchanged for European manufactures, increased world trade and brought untold wealth to Europe. For the production of these raw materials and articles of commerce Negro slaves were transported to the New World and became the main support of the "triangular trade" involving the metropolis, Africa, and the colonies. Negro slaves thus became the creators of the wealth that made the flowering of capitalism possible in the nineteenth century.[3]

## 1. Negro Slavery and the Plantation

In the southern sections of what became the United States, the plantation system of agriculture developed on the basis of enslaved Negro labor. After the failure of the attempt to utilize the native Indian as a source of forced labor, white indentured servants were introduced into the colonies.[4] But they were soon supplanted by Negro slaves, who proved a more efficient and a more economical source of labor. During the seventeenth and eighteenth centuries the importation of Negroes gradually increased to meet the growing need for laborers in the production of tobacco, rice, and indigo. But with the invention of the cotton gin, which enabled American producers to supply the increased demands of English manufacturers, the importation of Negro slaves was accelerated. As a result, the agitation against slavery, which had found expression along with the idealism

* Superior numbers refer to notes beginning on p. 197.

respecting liberty during the American Revolution, died down when the declining productivity of slave labor on tobacco plantations was followed by a period of unprecedented profits in cotton production.

The condition of the Negro slaves on the southern plantations varied considerably. In the lower South, where the large cotton plantation tended to take on the character of a purely industrial organization, the treatment of the slaves was extremely brutal since they were regarded as mere work animals. They were treated even more inhumanely by the slave traders who supplied the needs of a commercial system of agriculture. As articles of commerce, the Negro slaves were treated in the same manner as the mules which were advertised for sale along with them. On the other hand, where the plantation became a social as well as an economic organization, under a semi-patriarchal regime, more consideration was shown for the personalities of the slaves. The lives of the masters and slaves became intertwined in a system of social relationships. The relations between whites and blacks thus came to be regulated by a complex system of social rituals and etiquette permitting a maximum degree of intimacy while maintaining the complete subordination of the blacks. The traditions governing race relations on the plantation became so firmly rooted in the South that they have persisted until the present day.[5]

## 2. The Impact of Western Civilization

Where the plantation acquired the character of a social institution, it provided the means by which the Negro slaves could rapidly take over European culture. The basis for the rapid acculturation of the Negro slaves was created by the manner in which the slaves had been captured in Africa, sold on the slave markets, and integrated into the plantation system. The Negro slaves, who represented many different tribal backgrounds, had been captured in Africa during tribal wars and slave-hunting expeditions. They had been herded into the *baracoons* on the coast to await the arrival of slave ships. Then, during the Middle Passage they were transported in ships, in which they were packed spoon-fashion, to the West Indies where they were sold on the slave markets. In the West Indies they underwent a period of being "broken into" slavery before they were shipped to local plantations or to the plantations on the mainland. In the English colonies on the mainland, and later in the United States, they were widely scattered on plantations which had fewer slaves on the whole than did the plantations in the West Indies.

On the plantations in the southern states the Negro slave sloughed off almost completely his African cultural heritage.[6] The African family system was destroyed and the slave was separated from his kinsmen and friends. Moreover, in the United States there was little chance that he could reknit the ties of kinship and old associations. If by chance he encountered fellow slaves with whom he could communicate in his native tongue, he was separated from them. From the very beginning he was forced to learn English in order to obey the commands of his white masters. Whatever memories he might have retained of his native land and native customs became meaningless in the New World. The very fact that the majority of the slaves were young males practically eliminated the possibility of recreating a social organization that could perpetuate and transmit the African cultural heritage.

While all of the slaves were always under the surveillance of the whites, the house servants lived constantly in close association with their masters. Very often these house servants had associated from childhood with their masters. Consequently, they early acquired the speech of their masters, a fact which set them off from the more isolated field hands, who spoke a dialect. Living in close association with whites, the house servants were subject to a type of discipline which caused them to identify themselves with their masters. This discipline included both moral and religious instruction. The slaves participated in the religious life of their white masters—including family prayers and attendance at the white churches, where a section was reserved for them.

Some recognition had to be given the individual qualities

of the slaves, and it was most often among the house servants that these differences were recognized. For example, there was a division of labor on the plantation in which the intelligence and talents of the slaves found expression. Generally, the son of a house servant was apprenticed to some artisan to learn a skilled trade. These skilled mechanics, who constituted a large section of the artisans in the South, formed with the house servants a sort of privileged class in the slave community. The greater the integration of the slaves into the activities and family life of their white masters, the more nearly their behavior and ideals approximated those of the whites. On the other hand, the field hands, who had few intimate contacts with the whites and were subject to a more formal type of social control, could give expression to a more spontaneous type of behavior—especially in their religious life and in their musical creations. The field hands were especially attracted by the Methodist and Baptist missionaries who, in their revival meetings, preached a simple doctrine of salvation through conversion in which a highly emotional experience was of primary importance. Although the slaves were under the surveillance of the whites in order to prevent conspiracies and revolts, they were able to engage in a form of worship different from that of the whites and the more disciplined house servants. The Spirituals, or religious folksongs, grew out of these relatively independent religious meetings. The new slaves who were brought to the plantations from Africa had to adjust to a social world quite different from that from which they had come.

The close association of the races on the plantation, especially in the same household, resulted in considerable race mixture. The interbreeding of the races had begun in the seventeenth century soon after the introduction of Negroes into Virginia, and continued on a large scale as long as slavery existed. Many of the mulattoes were emancipated by their white fathers and formed the basis of the free Negro population that grew up in the South before the Civil War.[7] In 1850, mulattoes or mixed-bloods constituted 37 per cent of the free Negro population but only 8 per cent of the slave population.

The free Negroes were not evenly distributed over the South, but were concentrated principally in cities and in those states where the plantation system of agriculture did not flourish. In Maryland and Virginia, where there were 83,942 and 58,042 free Negroes, respectively, in 1860,[8] many of these free Negroes owed their freedom to the fact that they had been permitted to "hire their time" and work as semi-free laborers. With the money which they were able to accumulate after paying their masters for their "time" they bought their freedom. Although the majority of the free Negroes in the South did not live much above a subsistence level, many of them bought land and became independent farmers, or became successful mechanics and skilled artisans. In Charleston, South Carolina, and in New Orleans, the free Negroes or "free people of color" accumulated considerable wealth as skilled artisans, and as owners of plantations included slaves among their possessions.[9]

The free Negroes constituted, in fact, the element in the Negro population that had made the greatest progress in acquiring European culture. The pattern of family life of the well-to-do free Negroes in the plantation South was the same as the patriarchal family pattern of the slaveholding whites. Moreover, their outlook on life and their values were the same as the white models. They occupied the position of an intermediate caste in some parts of the South, especially in New Orleans. As a group the free Negroes of the South were much better off economically than the free Negroes of the North, who had not been able to compete with the European immigrants. At one time the free Negroes in the South outnumbered the free Negroes in the North, but as the result of persecutions following the antislavery agitation in the North many of them migrated to the North. Nevertheless, half of the nearly 500,000 free Negroes in the United States at the outbreak of the Civil War were in the South.

## 3. A Nation within a Nation?

As the result of the Civil War and Emancipation, the future status of the Negro in American society became one of the most pressing problems facing the American government. This problem was tied up with the problem of re-integrating the southern states into the federal Union. Lincoln, although opposed to slavery, had never believed that Negroes and whites could be citizens of the same community. He had cautiously suggested that the educated free mulattoes in Louisiana who had fought on the Union side should be permitted to qualify as citizens in the reconstructed government of Louisiana. The assassination of Lincoln followed too soon for him to make known his general program for the future of the Negro. The successor of Lincoln, Andrew Jackson, who as a representative of the non-slaveholding "poor whites" had remained loyal to the Union, soon made it clear that he wanted to build a "democracy" in the South consisting only of white citizens, or white men of property. As the result of this policy, he was opposed by two factions of the Republican Party— the abolitionists among the Old Radicals, who were genuinely interested in creating a democracy in the South based upon the political participation of whites and Negroes; and the Republicans who, fearing that a white farming class would nullify the victory of the North, wanted to use Negro voters to support legislation that would give a legal basis to triumphant industrial capitalism.[10]

The program of the Republican Congress for the reconstruction of the southern states gave promise of a democratic revolution in an area that had been ruled by a slaveholding oligarchy. Under the protection of the Union Army, the black freedmen along with the non-slaveholding whites were given the right to vote and hold office. Three amendments to the federal Constitution were necessary, however, to provide a legal basis for the citizenship of the Negro: the Thirteenth, abolishing slavery; the Fourteenth, making him a citizen; and the Fifteenth, forbidding restrictions upon his rights as a citizen on account of race or his previous status as a slave. Some of the more radical Republicans proposed that the plantations be divided in order to create a class of black and white small landowners. In fact, the black freedmen had been promised land by the federal government as a guarantee of their freedom. But since this program appeared too revolutionary for the majority of the Republican leaders, the vast majority of ex-slaves remained landless, except for a relatively small number of Negroes who had secured land during the Civil War.

The Negro has been blamed for the disorders and the graft on the part of politicians and speculators during the Reconstruction Period. But unprejudiced historians, who place the behavior of the Negro during this period in its proper perspective, agree that the Negro was the victim of the conflict of economic interests over which he had no control and that he exhibited considerable wisdom in attempting to help formulate social policies.[11] The Negro gave his support to the establishment of a system of public education and sought to make land available to the great masses of black and white farmers. But the question of race was utilized to divide the whites and Negroes. The "redemption" of the South in 1876, which was hailed as the restoration of "white supremacy," really resulted in the political ascendancy of the "Bourbons," or the new middle classes and the planters. The state constitutions, which were supposed to be the legal instruments by which the "barbarous blacks" maintained their power but were, in fact, nothing more than the expression of middle-class interests, were retained for decades after the restoration of "white supremacy."

The restoration of "white supremacy" did not resolve the class conflict among whites in the South. In fact, the white planters sometimes used Negro voters to defeat the aspirations of the disinherited whites. When agrarian unrest among the "poor whites" of the South joined forces with the Populist movement, which represented the general unrest among American farmers, the question of race was used to defeat the co-operation of "poor whites" and

Negroes. It was then that the demagogues assumed leadership of the "poor whites" and provided a solution to the class conflict among whites that offered no challenge to the political power and economic privileges of the industrialists and the planter class. The program, which made the Negro the scapegoat, contained the following provisions: (1) the Negro was completely disfranchised by all sorts of legal subterfuges, with the threat of force in the background; (2) the funds which were appropriated on a per capita basis for Negro school children were diverted to white schools; and (3) a legal system of segregation in all phases of public life was instituted. In order to justify this program, the demagogues, who were supported by the white propertied classes, engaged for twenty-five years in a campaign to prove that the Negro was subhuman, morally degenerate, and intellectually incapable of being educated.[12]

The North acquiesced in this program as a solution of the race problem. The rise to prominence of Booker T. Washington as the leader of the Negroes from 1895 onward was due to his apparent acceptance of racial segregation as a solution of the "Negro problem." Under his leadership, support of so-called "industrial education" for the Negro was provided by northern capitalists. During the quarter of a century from 1890 to 1915, when lynchings and mob violence were used to put the Negro "in his place" in the South, Negroes gave up their hope for freedom and equality in American life. Only a small group of northern Negro intellectuals, led by W. E. Burghardt Dubois and a few northern white "radicals" (on racial issues), attacked the so-called "solution" of the race problem. But more important than the attack of the radicals were changes in race relations which were set in motion by the northward migration of the Negro masses that began in 1915 as a result of the first World War.

But before analyzing the changes which occurred in race relations as the result of the northern migrations, let us consider the nature of the social world of the Negro which emerged as the result of the system of racial segregation.[13] Until the first World War only about a tenth of the Negroes in the United States were in the North, and seven-eighths of those in the North lived in cities. The residents of the relatively small Negro communities in the northern cities gained their livelihood in domestic and personal service. Although they were restricted in their opportunities for employment in industry and white-collar occupations, they did not suffer much discrimination in utilizing public institutions. However, they had their own churches and their social life revolved chiefly about their own clubs and other organizations. In the South, on the other hand, the entire life of the Negro—except for his contacts with whites as a domestic or personal servant, or as a laborer—was restricted to the Negro community. Although this rigid system of racial segregation grew up in a region where, until 1920, more than three-fourths of the Negroes lived on farms and plantations, the "color line" in southern cities was as rigid as in rural areas. In the rural areas the majority of the Negroes worked as sharecroppers under a system closely resembling serfdom, while the majority of those in the cities gained a livelihood as domestic servants and as unskilled laborers. The church was the chief center of the Negro's social life in both the cities and in the rural areas. It provided the chief means for self-expression and leadership and erected a shelter against a hostile white world. In conjunction with the church there were the numerous mutual aid societies and fraternal organizations that offered not only an opportunity for social life, but provided aid in the time of sickness and death.

In this segregated world, especially in cities, a class structure slowly emerged which was based upon social distinctions such as education and conventional behavior, rather than upon occupation and income. At the top of the social pyramid there was a small upper class. The superior status of this class was due chiefly to its differentiation from the great mass of the Negro population because of a family heritage which resulted partly from its mixed ancestry. The family heritage consisted of traditions of civilized behavior and economic efficiency. The members' light skin-color was indicative not only of their white ancestry, but of their descent from the Negroes who were free before the Civil War, or those who had enjoyed the advantages of having served in the houses of their masters. This upper class constantly incorporated those Negroes who were able to acquire an education in the schools supported by northern philanthropy. The members of the upper class depended on a number of skilled occupations for a living, though there was a sprinkling of teachers, doctors, educated ministers, and small businessmen among them.

It was from this isolated social world that thousands of Negroes began migrating to northern industrial centers during the first World War.[14] Although the migrants were attracted to northern cities because of opportunities for employment, the migrations were, in part, a flight from oppression to a Promised Land of freedom and equality. But many of the Negro migrants became disillusioned about the North when, without neighbors and friends, they faced the keen competition and racial discrimination of the cold, impersonal environment of northern cities. In their disillusionment many of them joined the Garvey Movement, the only serious Negro nationalist movement to arise in the United States. According to the leader of this movement, Marcus Garvey, who was a Negro of West Indian origin, the Negro would never achieve equality in America, a white man's country, and therefore the only salvation for the Negro was to return to Africa. Negro intellectuals and the middle-class Negroes generally were hostile to this movement, which gradually dissolved when the leader was sent to the federal penitentiary in Atlanta.[15]

Despite the failure of the Negro to find a Promised Land in the North, the Negro enjoyed certain advantages in the North that changed his outlook on the world as well as his status in American society. In the North the Negro worker gained a foothold for the first time in American industry. Negro children had access for the first time on a large scale to a standard American education, generally in nonsegregated schools. Negroes enjoyed the right to vote and hold office, and as the result of their political power could resist racial discrimination. Through their experience with city life, Negroes acquired a certain sophistication towards the world and tended to redefine their problems in America. They did not seek a solution in a narrow program of racial exclusiveness such as the Garvey Movement. Especially during the Depression years some of them joined the Communist Party, which defined the Negro problem as a problem of "national liberation" from capitalist oppression.[16] The vast majority of Negroes, however, gave up their sentimental allegiance to the Republican Party and supported the Democratic Party and the New Deal Program, which offered concrete economic advantages and a promise of satisfying their aspirations as citizens.

The greater economic and social freedom of the North accelerated the slow occupational differentiation of the Negro population. The rise of the industrial unions (C.I.O.) with their more liberal racial policy helped the integration of Negro workers into industry.[17] But workers did not share immediately in the benefits of the economic revival that followed the decision of the United States to become the "arsenal of democracy." It was the result of agitation and the demand for manpower in a war against Nazism with its racial policy, that the Negro began to enjoy some of the fruits of an expanding American economy. Since the second World War, Negroes have continued to receive a larger share of the national income than they did before the War. Moreover, the racial barriers in the North, where nearly a third of the Negroes now live, have tended to be lowered in all phases of public life. Even in the South, the segregation of the Negro has been less rigid in public transportation, and Negro students have been admitted to some of the public universities. As the result of the changes in the economic status of the Negro, the Negro middle class, or the "black bourgeoisie" has grown in size and acquired a dominant position among Negroes.

## 4. Purpose of the Present Study

The primary purpose of this study is to make a sociological analysis of the behavior, the attitudes, and values
of the "black bourgeoisie," a group which began to play
an important role among American Negroes during the
past two decades. Our analysis will deal with two aspects
of the life of the "black bourgeoisie"—the first being the
real or objectively existing economic condition and social
status of the "black bourgeoisie" in the United States, and
the second being the standards of behavior and values of
the isolated social world of this segment of the Negro
population, which has come into existence as a consequence
of racial discrimination and racial segregation.

The first part of this study, which deals with the real
status of the black bourgeoisie, will be concerned, first,
with the process by which a black bourgeoisie has emerged
in the United States as the result of a slow and difficult occupational differentiation of the Negro population.
Against this background will be analyzed the present
economic basis of this class, especially as regards the recent changes that have occurred in the economic position
of the Negro in the American economy. The study of the
economic position of the black bourgeoisie will include
a realistic appraisal of the significance of "Negro business"
in the American economy as well as in the economic life
of the Negro. In this part of the study attention will also
be given to the education of the Negro, since education
has been the principal social factor responsible for the
emergence of the black bourgeoisie. Special attention will
be directed to the influence of the segregated schools and
colleges on the aspirations and social outlook of the black
bourgeoisie. Our analysis will be directed next to the political outlook of this class and the power which the black
bourgeoisie exercises over Negroes—since the same economic and social forces in American life, which have been
largely responsible for the existence of "Negro education"
have shaped the political orientation of the black bourgeoisie.

The concluding chapter of the first part will deal with what, from a sociological standpoint, has been one of the most important consequences of the emergence of the black bourgeoisie, namely, the uprooting of this stratum of the Negro population from its "racial" traditions or, more specifically, from its folk background. As the result of the break with its cultural past, the black bourgeoisie is without cultural roots in either the Negro world with which it refuses to identify, or the white world which refuses to permit the black bourgeoisie to share its life. This chapter will provide a transition to the second part of the study, which will be devoted to the behavior of the black bourgeoisie in the social world that has grown up out of its isolation in American life.

Lacking a cultural tradition and rejecting identification with the Negro masses on the one hand, and suffering from the contempt of the white world on the other, the black bourgeoisie has developed a deep-seated inferiority complex. In order to compensate for this feeling of inferiority, the black bourgeoisie has created in its isolation what might be described as a world of make-believe in which it attempts to escape the disdain of whites and fulfill its wish for status in American life. One of the most striking indications of the unreality of the social world which the black bourgeoisie created is its faith in the importance of "Negro business," i.e., the business enterprises owned by Negroes and catering to Negro customers. Although these enterprises have little significance either from the standpoint of the American economy or the economic life of the Negro, a social myth has been created that they provide a solution to the Negro's economic problems. Faith in this social myth and others is perpetuated by the Negro newspapers, which represent the largest and most successful business enterprises established by Negroes. Moreover, the Negro newspapers help to create and maintain the world of make-believe in which Negroes can realize their desires for recognition and status in a white world that regards them with contempt and amusement. Much of the news featured in the Negro newspapers is concerned with the activities of the members of Negro "society," or it tends to make "socialites" out of most Negroes whose activities are considered newsworthy. "Society" is a phase of the world of make-believe which represents in an acute form the Negro's long preoccupation with "social life" as an escape from his subordinate status in America.

Since the world of make-believe can not insulate the black bourgeoisie completely from the world of reality, the members of this class exhibit considerable confusion and conflict in their personalities. Their emotional and mental conflicts arise partly from their constant striving for status within the Negro world, as well as in the estimation of whites. Moreover, they have accepted unconditionally the values of the white bourgeois world: its morals and its canons of respectability, its standards of beauty and consumption. In fact, they have tended to overemphasize their conformity to white ideals. Nevertheless, they are rejected by the white world, and this rejection has created considerable self-hatred, since it is attributed to their Negro characteristics. At the same time, because of their ambivalence towards Negroes, they are extremely sensitive to slights and discriminations which Negroes suffer. Since they do not truly identify themselves with Negroes, the hollowness of the black bourgeoisie's pretended "racial pride" is revealed in the value which it places upon a white or light complexion. Because of their social isolation and lack of a cultural tradition, the members of the black bourgeoisie in the United States seem to be in the process of becoming NOBODY. What significance, then, does the fate of the black bourgeoisie in the United States have for the bourgeoisie of other racial or cultural minorities that have come into existence as the result of the expansion of western civilization and European capitalism?

# PART ONE
# THE WORLD OF REALITY

# Chapter I

## The Roots of the Black Bourgeoisie

IF ONE WOULD ferret out the roots of the black bourgeoisie in the United States, one would have to study the varied and sporadic efforts of the Negroes who were free before the Civil War to acquire wealth. However, it was not until after Emancipation that the spirit of modern business enterprise really took root among the Negro elite. This was due to their association with the Freedmen's Bank, which was established to encourage thrift among the newly emancipated slaves. While the initiation of the Negro elite in the field of business enterprise ended with the failure of the Freedmen's Bank, the spirit of business enterprise engendered by this experience was never lost. Whereas an increasing number of Negroes continued to set up small stores and shops and a few larger undertakings, primarily to serve the needs of the segregated Negro communities, it was mainly in the field of banking that the new spirit of business enterprise manifested itself. Negro leaders in all areas of community life—education, religion, and fraternal organizations—began to organize their own banks in a number of cities of the South.

### 1. Efforts of the Free Negroes to Acquire Wealth

Before the Civil War, the ownership of land or real estate was the main avenue open to the free Negro who undertook to acquire wealth.[1] During the latter years of the eighteenth century, following the American Revolution, free Negroes began to acquire land in New York and Pennsylvania. Some of the free Negroes who migrated from the South gradually acquired land in southern Ohio during the early decades of the nineteenth century. In those areas of the upper South which were not dominated by the plantation system, some free Negroes were even able to acquire land despite the general opposition to their presence. As the plantation system of agriculture became unprofitable in the Tidewater section in Maryland because of the exhaustion of the soil, the plantations were broken up into small farms and some of the growing numbers of free Negroes were able to buy small farms in the poorer sections of this area. The plantation system was also dying out in the Tidewater section of Virginia for the same reason as in Maryland, and the free Negro population was increasing.[2] In 1830 the free Negroes owned about 32,000 acres of land valued at $184,184, and by 1860 both the acreage and the value of the farms owned by free Negroes had doubled.[3] Since nearly half (43 per cent) of the farms owned by the 1,200 free Negro farm owners contained 25 acres or less, it may be assumed that these farms were used for subsistence rather than for commercial enterprises. In North Carolina, where the plantation system was never as extensive as in states farther south, a small number of free Negroes acquired land.[4] Slightly more than 10 per cent, or 3,659 of the 30,463 free Negroes in the state, were listed as owners of property in 1860, 1,211 of whom owned real estate having a total value of $480,986. It was only in Louisiana, where under French rule a considerable class of free mulattoes or *gens de couleur* had become important, that free Negroes owned large plantations with slaves.[5] The value of some of these plantations ranged from $40,000 to $200,000 and they had from 40 to 100 slaves.[6]

In the cities of the North as well as of the South, the free Negroes were able to accumulate some wealth through the ownership of real estate. The free Negroes in Philadelphia owned nearly 100 houses before 1800, and by 1856 their real estate holdings were valued at $800,000.[7] In 1853 it was reported at a convention of colored people in Rochester that Negroes owned over a million dollars in real estate in New York City.[8] By 1840 the free Negroes in Cincinnati, Ohio, had accumulated $228,000 in real estate.[9] The real estate holdings of the free Negroes in the District of Columbia amounted to $630,000, and in Baltimore about a half million dollars at the opening of the Civil War.[10] Among the taxpayers in Charleston, South Carolina, in 1860, there were listed 371 free persons of color, including 13 Indians, who paid taxes on real estate valued at about a million dollars and 389 slaves.[11] In New Orleans, where the free Negroes or *gens de couleur* were better off economically and socially than in other parts of the South, their holdings in real estate and slaves were estimated to be from ten to fifteen million dollars in 1860.[12]

Except in Louisiana, the majority of the nearly 4,000 Negroes in the United States who owned slaves lived in urban communities.[13] In many cases the Negro owners of slaves had bought a wife or husband, a brother or sister, or children, who were slaves and who thus became legally slaves of the Negro who bought them. Although it is impossible to say what proportion of the Negro owners of slaves bought them for philanthropic motives, those free Negroes who owned plantations or maintained large estates in Charleston and New Orleans owned slaves for the same reason as the white slaveholders. Moreover, it appears that in the cities the Negro owners of slaves were often motivated, as the white owners, by profit in buying and selling slaves.

But slaves were relatively a small part of the personal property which the free Negroes were able to accumulate in cities. In the cities where the free Negroes were able to engage in a number of occupations, they managed to accumulate some capital and engage in business undertakings.[14] In the southern cities the free Negro artisans provided much of the skilled labor. Among the 700 employed free Negro males in Charleston, South Carolina, in 1850, there were 122 carpenters, 87 tailors, 30 shoemakers, 14 wheelwrights, 18 bricklayers, 23 butchers, 10 bootmakers, 14 millwrights, and 11 painters. Free Negroes were found in a larger number of skilled occupations in New Orleans than in any other city of the country. In addition to the occupations enumerated for Charleston, South Carolina, the free Negroes or *gens de couleur* were listed in 1850 as bookbinders, cabinet makers, cigarmakers, masons, coopers, sailmakers, architects, brokers, clerks, teachers, and capitalists. Although the skilled Negro workers did not occupy in northern cities the same strategic position as in southern cities, a few of them were to be found in a large number of occupations. They were to be found in small numbers in most of the occupations listed for the free Negroes in Charleston, South Carolina and in New Orleans. But they were not found in such occupations as architects, bookbinders, brickmakers, cabinet makers, masons, upholsterers, or the occupations in which they would meet the keen competition of immigrant European labor. A relatively large proportion of the free Negroes in the northern areas had to depend upon domestic and personal service for a living.

Some of the free Negro artisans in cities worked independently and set up small businesses. In addition to the twenty-one Negroes who were listed in Boston in 1850 as traders, there were tailors, hairdressers and barbers who worked independently. The free Negroes in New York City owned a newspaper, a dyeing establishment, a drugstore, small stores, and restaurants.[15] There were among the most successful Negro businessmen in Philadelphia a sail manufacturer, a broker, and a lumber merchant.[16] In the cities of Virginia the free Negroes worked independently as blacksmiths, millers, boat men, restaurant operators, tavern keepers, and grocerymen.[17] As we have seen, in New Orleans free Negroes were listed not only as tailors, cigarmakers, and blacksmiths, occupations in which they worked independently, but as merchants, brokers, and capitalists. The business operations of the free Negro extended beyond these occupational groups. For example, the free Negroes in New Orleans, as in other southern cities, accumulated money as draymen, or in the field of transportation, because this was a type of business in which white men did not enter. Then they amassed wealth in those occupations and businesses associated with cooking. In both northern and southern cities they operated taverns for whites, and in New York and Philadelphia a number of Negro caterers achieved financial success as well as renown in their professions. There were still other ways in which the free Negroes were able to accumulate wealth. Because of their precarious economic position in cities, the free Negroes organized mutual aid societies. These societies not only provided mutual aid, but encouraged saving and the accumulation of wealth. In a number of cities there were individual Negroes who engaged in money lending, using the wealth which they had accumulated as a barber or carpenter for capital.

It has been estimated that the free Negroes accumulated $50,000,000 in real and personal wealth before the Civil War.[18] The savings and business undertakings on the part of the free Negroes reflected the spirit and values of their environment. Through thrift and saving, white American artisans hoped to accumulate wealth and get ahead. This spirit was encouraged among the free Negroes by their leaders, one of the most distinguished of whom has been described as a "black Benjamin Franklin."[19] In fact, these free Negroes were trained in the "old style" bourgeois spirit represented by Benjamin Franklin.[20] It was not until after Emancipation that the new bourgeois spirit would take hold among the leaders of the freedmen.

## 2. The Freedmen's Savings Bank

During the Civil War a number of banks were established in order to enable Negro soldiers to save all or part of the "allotments" which the government made to them or their families.[21] As the War drew to a close, an army paymaster and a Congregational minister, who had served as an army chaplain, devised a plan for setting up a bank in order to encourage thrift on the part of the newly emancipated blacks. As the result of their efforts, an act was passed by Congress and signed by Abraham Lincoln on March 3, 1865, providing for the establishment of the Freedmen's Savings Bank. According to the Congressional act, the purpose of the bank was to receive deposits offered "by or in behalf of persons heretofore held in slavery in the United States, or their descendants."[22] It was also stated in the act creating the bank that any interest un-

called for in two years should be used for the education
of Negro children. Although, according to the act, it appeared that the bank was to restrict its activities to the
District of Columbia, branches were set up in various parts
of the country.[23] Within less than a year ten branches were
set up, and at the end of 1866 ten more branches were
established. During the period of its expansion, a total of
thirty-four branches were established, thirty-two of which
were in the South. The rapid expansion was due to a
campaign which was carried on among the ex-slaves. They
were told that the bank had the backing of Lincoln and
were given the impression, at least, that it was guaranteed
by the Congress and government of the United States.
Moreover, the fact that the bank was a benevolent institution established for the ex-slaves was emphasized in order
to secure the deposits of Negroes.

Despite the enthusiastic support which Negroes gave to
the bank, this support being reflected in the rapid accumulation of deposits, the bank began to run into difficulties.
These difficulties were due partly to certain weaknesses in
the organization of the bank. Those responsible for the
bank were not legally bound by the charter of the bank nor
did they have any financial interest in the institution.
Moreover, during the rapid expansion of the bank some of
the branches which were set up became a liability. As long
as the headquarters of the bank was in New York, it was
conducted by businessmen who regarded their responsibility as a public trust. But when the headquarters was
moved to Washington it was placed in the hands of in-
competent missionaries and speculators. However, in ac-
counting for the failure of the bank, one must take into
account also the hostility of southern whites and the fact
that the failure of the bank was one incident among many
others in the reckless expansion during the post-Civil War
period which ended in the panic of 1873.[24]

When the Freedmen's Savings Bank was on the verge
of failure, Frederick Douglass, who after escaping from
slavery became the leading abolitionist orator of the day
and later the greatest leader of the Negroes, was made

president of the bank. Douglass, who thought that the bank was sound, believed he could save this symbol of the Negro's achievement of equality in American life. In his autobiography he wrote:

About four months before this splendid institution was compelled to close its doors in the starved and deluded faces of its depositors, and while I was assured by its President and by its Actuary of its sound condition, I was solicited by some of its trustees to allow them to use my name in the board as a candidate for its Presidency. So I waked up one morning to find myself seated in a comfortable arm chair, with gold spectacles on my nose, and to hear myself addressed as President of the Freedmen's Bank. I could not help reflecting on the contrast between Frederick the slave boy, running about at Col. Lloyd's with only a tow linen shirt to cover him, and Frederick—President of a Bank—counting its assets by millions. I had heard of golden dreams, but such dreams had no comparison with this reality. And yet this seeming reality was scarcely more substantial than a dream. My term of service on this golden height covered only the brief space of three months, and these three months were divided into two parts, during the first part of which I was quietly employed in an effort to find out the real condition of the Bank and its numerous branches. This was no easy task. On paper, and from the representations of its management, its assets amounted to three millions of dollars, and its liabilities were about equal to its assets.[25]

Douglass undertook to save the bank by instituting economies and by closing the branches that were a liability. He was so confident of the soundness of the bank that he lent it $10,000 of his own money. Despite the efforts of Douglass the bank was finally forced to close in 1874. During the six years which were required to liquidate the assets of the bank, 40 per cent of the deposits were paid to the principal depositors, while the majority of small depositors failed to receive dividends either because they could not be located or they had given up hope of recovering their deposits.

Although Negro leaders once made the dubious claim that the failure of the Freedman's Savings Bank destroyed the faith of Negroes in banks and discouraged thrift among them,[26] the bank succeeded nevertheless in giving Negroes training in business and in implanting in them bourgeois ideals. The literature distributed by the bank was designed to teach them how their savings would increase through interest and how thrift would bring them the things they desired.[27] Booklets containing pictures and poems, which provided homely advice on thrift as the means to riches, were widely distributed among Negroes. Gradually Negro clerks and officials were employed in the various branches of the bank and Negroes were made advisers and directors of the institution. Douglass' recollection of the pride and amazement which he felt in seeing Negro clerks in the main branch of the bank in Washington gives some indication of what the bank symbolized in the aspirations of the Negro to conform to American ideals.

In passing it on the street I often peeped into its spacious windows, and looked down the row of its gentlemanly and elegantly dressed colored clerks, with their pens behind their ears and buttonhole bouquets in their coat-fronts, and felt my very eyes enriched. It was a sight I had never expected to see. I was amazed with the facility with which they counted the money; they threw off the thousands with dexterity, if not the accuracy, of old and experienced clerks. The whole thing was beautiful. I had read of this Bank when I lived in Rochester, and had indeed been solicited to become one of its trustees, and had reluctantly consented to do so; but when I came to Washington and saw its magnificent brown stone front, its towering height, and its perfect appointments, and the fine display it made in the transaction of its business, I felt like the Queen of Sheba when she saw the riches of Solomon, "the half had not been told me."[28]

## 3. Independent Ventures in the Field of Banking

The spirit of business enterprise which had been implanted among Negroes by the Freedmen's Savings Bank began to blossom forth within fifteen years after the failure of that institution. Beginning in 1888, Negroes organized at least 134 banks between that year and 1934.[29] All over the South, during the years prior to 1910, banks organized by Negroes "sprang up like mushrooms but died almost as rapidly as they were organized."[30] In 1888 Negroes organized two banks, the Savings Bank of the Grand Fountain of United Order of True Reformers in Richmond, Virginia, and the Capital Savings Bank in Washington, D. C. During the following year the Mutual Trust Company was organized in Chattanooga, Tennessee, and in 1890 the Alabama Penny Savings and Loan Company was established in Birmingham, Alabama. Within the seven years from 1899 to 1905, at least twenty-eight banks were opened in various southern cities by Negroes.[31] But at the end of 1905, of all the banks organized by Negroes, only seven were still in existence.[32]

The widespread and numerous ventures of Negroes in the field of banking were due to a number of causes, both economic and social. The majority of the early attempts to set up banks were designed to provide depositories for the funds which were accumulated by the fraternal organizations. These fraternal organizations, together with the "sickness and burial" societies, began to flourish after the emancipation of the Negro.[33] This was owing to the fact that following Emancipation, the Negro was dependent upon his own resources and initiative and therefore co-operation for mutual aid in meeting the crises of life became necessary. At the same time, the ex-slaves had been taught the ideals of thrift and saving by the Yankee missionaries who had gone into the South to establish schools for the freedmen. The spirit of business enterprise, which had been at the basis of the propaganda carried on by the promoters of the Freedmen's Bank, became an article of faith, as we shall see later, after the Negro lost his political rights and was gradually eliminated from skilled occupations.

The circumstances under which the first Negro bank, the True Reformer Bank, as it was known, was organized in 1888, will throw light on the problems which the pioneer Negro businessmen undertook to solve through business enterprise.[34] The United Order of True Reformers was founded in 1876 by a former slave (who had become a preacher) in order to provide sick and death benefits for its members. As the result of a lynching, followed by rumors that the whites were planning to destroy one of the lodges of the Order which had entrusted its funds with a white storekeeper, it was decided that the Order should establish a bank as a depository for its funds. The funds of the bank were to be used to finance stores, a hotel and other enterprises of the Order; to support a home for aged Negroes; and to finance a rural enterprise including the raising and marketing of agricultural products, and a Negro community. From the account of this rural enterprise as given by an officer of the Order, one may see how the faith in business enterprise was mingled with the Negro's religious faith.

> The farm consisted of six hundred and thirty-four and one-quarter acres of land. In September, 1889, one hundred and thirty lots were cut off and offered for sale. Notwithstanding the gloom of darkness that hung densely over the project, those of faith rallied to the flag, and many lots were sold. Some paid cash in full and others paid in part. All of this was done by faith. God sent men of means with an electric car line, terminating at the boundary of the farm, which links Richmond and Westham together, and doubly increased the value of the land. All of these things are evidences of God's goodness and His acquiescence in the good work. This Negro settlement is destined to be the finest place of resort and pleasure of the Southland. It is called "Browneville," in honor of the founder of the Order. In 1902 every lot had been sold.[35]

The bank conducted by this Order failed in 1910,

as many other banks did during this period and subsequently. The stores which were financed by the Order were operated at a heavy loss. Although the failure of the bank was due partly to the negligence and dishonesty of the management, its failure was foredoomed by the "unproductive use of its credit."[36] The failure of this bank as well as the failure of other ventures by Negroes in banking was due partly to their ignorance of banking principles. At the same time these failures indicate the difficulties faced by banks conducted by Negroes for the purpose of supporting "racial" business enterprises.

Negro banks were organized primarily to supply the Negro businessmen with credit and capital. But when one considers the nature of the Negro business enterprises for which Negro banks would supply credit and capital, the difficulty of conducting banks primarily for Negro enterprises becomes clear. Except for the insurance companies, the only outlets for the credit resources of Negro banks were in real estate, small and inconsequential retail stores, and the amusement and personal service enterprises conducted by Negroes. These enterprises do not offer an opportunity for the type of commercial transactions which are necessary for banking activities. Many a Negro bank which has failed possessed only frozen and depreciated real estate holdings among its most important assets. Negro leaders, not only those engaged in business, have asserted that the organization of Negro banks was necessary because of the refusal of white banks to grant credit and capital to Negroes. Although white banks because of racial prejudice have at times refused credit to Negro businessmen, the main reason for their refusal has been their understanding of the economic factors responsible for the failure of the Negro banks.

We may conclude our discussion of the origins of the black bourgeoisie with these remarks on Negro banks, since the banks have been the main symbols of the bourgeois spirit among Negroes. In the next chapter we shall turn our attention to an analysis of the present economic basis of this class in the Negro community.

# Chapter II

## The Economic Basis of Middle-Class Status

THE BLACK BOURGEOISIE is constituted of those Negroes who derive their incomes principally from the services which they render as white-collar workers. Despite the dreams of Negro leaders at the turn of the century that Negro businessmen would become organizers of big industries and large financial undertakings, Negroes have not become captains of industries nor even the managers of large corporations. Through the slow occupational differentiation of the Negro population, which was accelerated as the result of the migrations to northern cities and the changes in the American economy during two world wars, a class of white-collar workers has acquired a dominant position among Negroes. What has come to be known as "Negro business" has consisted chiefly, with the exception of a few insurance companies, of a number of small banks, and newspapers, of small retail stores, restaurants, undertaking establishments, and similar enterprises which serve the needs of the segregated Negro communities. Since the black bourgeoisie has always derived its income principally from white-collar occupations, we shall give attention first to the increasing occupational differentiation of the Negro population over the years.

## 1. Increasing Occupational Differentiation of the Negro Population

In 1900, when nine-tenths of the Negroes were still in the South, and four-fifths of those in the South lived in the rural areas, 60 per cent of the Negroes derived their living from agriculture. Ten years later the situation had changed only slightly, since 55 per cent continued to work on the soil.[1] By 1910 both the number and percentage of owners among Negro farmers had reached their maximum. One-fourth of the Negro farmers had managed to buy their farms while the other three-fourths were tenants, the majority of whom were mere sharecroppers.[2] The vast majority of Negro workers who were not in agriculture worked as unskilled laborers or in domestic service. A small professional group comprising between two and three per cent of all workers, and an even smaller group of clerical workers, had gradually become differentiated from the Negro masses.

A definite change occurred in the occupational distribution of the Negro population as the result of the northward migrations which began in 1915. By 1920 the proportion of Negroes in the North had increased to 14.1 per cent, and five-sixths of those in the North were in cities, principally large cities. In the South the number and proportion of Negroes in agriculture had declined markedly as the result of the movement of Negroes into the numerous small towns and cities of the South as well as to northern industrial centers.[3] The Negro migrants to southern cities tended to swell the number of Negroes who gained a living from unskilled labor and domestic service. On the other hand, in the northern cities Negroes began to enter occupations from which they had previously been barred. This was due to a number of reasons: the absence of a rigid color bar to the Negro's employment in certain types of occupations, better educational opportunities, the Negro's newly acquired political power, and a wider range of employment opportunities, including those created by the large Negro communities.[4] For example, in the South the only opportunity for clerical employment had been in a Negro business or in a Negro school, while in the North large numbers of Negroes were able to secure employment as clerks in public service as the result of the Negro's participation in political life. When the Depression broke in 1930, Negro workers in both northern and southern cities were forced out of their usual employment to a larger extent than white workers. Many of them were forced back into domestic service, but two-thirds of them continued to depend upon occupations outside of agriculture for a livelihood. Even in the South less than half of the employed Negroes were in agriculture. In the North the Negro workers had secured for the first time a foothold in American industry, and this foothold was not lost during the Depression. Moreover, in northern cities Negroes had an opportunity to participate in the various relief projects on the basis of their skills and education. Although the Depression tended to slow up the occupational differentiation of the Negro population, it did not stop it altogether.

The extent to which the Negro population had become differentiated occupationally by 1940 can be seen by studying the situation in the eleven cities in the United States which had Negro communities numbering 100,000 or more in 1940.[5] These eleven cities—four southern, three border and four northern—had a total Negro population of more than two million, with more than a million Negroes being in the four northern cities.[6] In the southern cities the small professional group accounted for only about three per cent of the employed males. The proprietors were relatively more numerous in northern cities than in southern cities. The most important difference appeared in regard to the clerical workers. In all of the northern cities the clerical workers constituted a much larger proportion of Negro workers than their same group in southern or border cities, with the exception of Washington. This is explained by the fact that in Washington a relatively large proportion of Negroes were employed in the federal government. The advantage enjoyed by northern cities was due to the reasons which we have indicated. There was little difference between northern cities and southern cities in regard to skilled craftsmen except in the case of Detroit, which had the largest percentage of skilled Negro craftsmen. In respect to skilled craftsmen both northern and southern cities had a larger proportion of this occupational group than border cities. But in northern cities a smaller percentage of Negroes were employed as common laborers than in southern and border cities.

On the basis of the occupational distribution of Negroes in these cities, it appeared that in southern and border cities the black bourgeoisie constituted about one-sixth of the Negro population, while in northern cities, it constituted a little more than a fifth of the Negro population. The Negro community in Washington, with a black bourgeoisie as large as northern cities, deviated from the border pattern because of the employment of Negroes in the federal government.

## 2. Occupational Status and Incomes

We may get a better idea of the size and character of the black bourgeoisie in the United States by considering the proportion of Negro male workers in those occupations from which the black bourgeoisie derives its income. This is shown for the employed male Negro population in Table I below. According to the figures in this table about one-sixth of the Negro men in the United States are employed in occupations which identify them with the black bourgeoisie. It will be observed, however, that the proportion of Negro men so employed in the

## Table I—Percentage of All Employed Negro Males in Four Major Occupations in 1950*

| Major Occupation Group | United States | South | North | West |
|---|---|---|---|---|
| Professional and Technical | 2.2 | 1.9 | 2.6 | 3.0 |
| Managers, Officials, and Proprietors | 2.1 | 1.7 | 3.0 | 2.8 |
| Clericals, Sales, etc. | 4.3 | 2.5 | 8.1 | 8.5 |
| Craftsmen, foremen, etc. | 7.7 | 6.3 | 10.7 | 10.3 |
| | 16.3 | 12.4 | 24.4 | 24.6 |

* Based upon U. S. Bureau of the Census, *U. S. Census of Population, 1950.* Vol. IV. *Special Reports,* Part 3, Chapter B, Nonwhite Population by Race, U. S. Government Printing Office, Washington, D. C. Table 9.

North and West is twice as great as in the South. This difference becomes even more significant when we consider the variations for the different occupational groups.

Beginning with the professional and technical group, we find that it is relatively small in all sections of the country, though it is larger in the North and West than in the South. The proportion of Negroes in professional and technical occupations is less than one-third as large as the proportion is among white Americans.[7] Among Negroes this group includes, principally, schoolteachers, preachers, physicians, dentists, lawyers, college professors, entertainers, embalmers, funeral directors, social workers, and nurses, and only a small sprinkling of persons in the technical occupations such as architecture, engineering and chemistry. But it should be pointed out that the Negro professional group in the North is represented by a much wider range of occupations—especially as regards technical occupations, in which Negroes are seldom found in the South. These same differences between the North and West on the one hand, and the South on the other, appear in the next occupational group, designated as managers, officials, and proprietors (exclusive of farm owners). In the white population one out of seven employed white males is in this occupational group, whereas only one in thirty employed Negro males in the North and West and only one in fifty in the South is in this category.[8] This occupational group includes buyers, postmasters, public administration officials, credit men, purchasing agents, shippers of farm products, railroad conductors and union officials as well as proprietors of business enterprises. Negroes are not permitted to work in a number of these occupations; for example, they cannot be railroad conductors because the Brotherhood of Railroad Conductors excludes all persons of Negro descent. In some of these occupations they may be found in small numbers because of exceptional circumstances.

The relative size of the black bourgeoisie in the Negro population has increased during the past decade largely because the proportion of Negro workers in clerical and kindred occupations has more than doubled and the proportion of female clerical workers quadrupled since 1940. In 1940 the proportion of employed Negro males in clerical and kindred fields was slightly more than two per cent and the proportion of employed females slightly more than one per cent. The significance of this sudden increase appears more striking when one considers it in relation to white workers in the same category. The proportion of Negro male workers in this category, which was one-fourth as large as white male workers in 1940, became one-half as large in 1950. During the same period the proportion of Negro female workers in clerical services, which was less than one-twentieth as large as that for white female workers, has become one-seventh as large. These changes must be considered in connection with the figures on the proportion of Negro clerical workers for the different regions of the United States as shown in Table I. The increase in the proportion of Negro men and women in clerical occupations has not occurred in the South, but in the North and the West. This group of occupations includes bank tellers, bookkeepers, cashiers, secretaries, stenographers, telephone and telegraph operators, mail carriers and railway mail clerks—all, with the exception of the last two, being occupations from which Negroes are barred in the South unless they work in a Negro school or Negro business establishment. During and especially since World War II, Negro men and women in the North have been entering clerical occupations, both in public and private employment, as the result of political pressure and the Fair Employment Practices Laws enacted in eleven states and twenty-five cities.

We come finally to the occupational group—craftsmen, foremen, and kindred workers—which constitutes on the whole the lower-middle class and is therefore identified with the black bourgeoisie. This group, which includes chiefly the skilled workers among Negroes, increased during World War II. In 1940 the proportion of Negro workers in this group was slightly more than one-third the proportion among white workers, whereas in 1950 the proportion of Negro workers in this category was almost one-half that of whites. While there was an increase in the proportion of craftsmen among Negro workers in the South as well as the North, the increase was greater in the North and this occupational group is relatively larger in the North.[9] The increase in craftsmen is due to the more liberal policy of the labor unions, especially in the North, as well as the laws which have been enacted recently against discrimination in employment.

It is not possible to secure exact information on the incomes of Negroes who constitute the black bourgeoisie. In 1949 the median income of Negro families in the United States was $1,665, or 51 per cent of the median income of white families, which was $3,232.[10] Only 16 per cent of the Negro families as compared with 55 per cent of the white families had incomes of $3,000 or more. There were important differences between regions, as one may see from the following table on the distribution of the incomes of all Negroes with incomes in 1949. The fact that 38.6 per cent of the Negro males in the South earn less than $500 a year as compared with 14.7 per cent in the North and 17.2 per cent in the West is due partly

### Table II—Percentage Distribution of the Incomes of Negroes with Incomes: 1949*

| Income | United States | South | North | West |
|---|---|---|---|---|
| Less than $500 | 30.6 | 38.6 | 14.7 | 17.2 |
| $500- $999 | 21.3 | 23.8 | 16.1 | 18.2 |
| 1,000-1,499 | 14.9 | 14.9 | 14.9 | 14.3 |
| 1,500-1,999 | 11.6 | 10.3 | 14.4 | 12.3 |
| 2,000-2,499 | 9.8 | 6.7 | 16.0 | 14.6 |
| 2,500-2,999 | 5.6 | 2.9 | 10.9 | 10.7 |
| 3,000-3,999 | 4.7 | 1.9 | 10.1 | 9.8 |
| 4,000-4,999 | 0.8 | 0.4 | 1.6 | 1.6 |
| 5,000-5,999 | 0.2 | 0.1 | 0.5 | 0.5 |
| 6,000 and over | 0.3 | 0.2 | 0.5 | 0.5 |

* Based upon U. S. Bureau of the Census, *U. S. Census of Population, 1950*, Vol. IV. *Special Reports*, Part 3, Chapter B, Nonwhite Population by Race. U. S. Government Printing Office, Washington, D. C., 1953, Table 9.

to the large number of Negroes in agriculture. But this is not the only explanation, since the median income of Negroes in southern cities was $861 as compared with $1,665 in northern cities. In Table II one can see the same significant differences between the incomes of Negroes in the North and West, and the South at all levels of incomes.

On the basis of the information given in Table II, it has been possible to estimate the incomes of Negroes who derive their incomes from the occupations in Table I.[11] For the country as a whole, the incomes of the members of the black bourgeoisie range from between $2,000 and $2,500 and upwards. The majority of their incomes do not amount to as much as $4,000. In fact, scarcely more than one per cent of all the Negroes in the country have an income amounting to $4,000 and only one-half of one per cent of them have an income of $5,000 or more. In the South the incomes of the black bourgeoisie begin at $2,000 and the majority of them do not reach $3,000. Only seven-tenths of one per cent, or seven Negroes in every thousand, with incomes in the South have incomes amounting to $4,000 or more. On the other hand, in the North and in the West the incomes of the black bourgeoisie begin at $2,500. Although the majority of their incomes are less than $4,000, nearly a half of them are between $3,000 and $4,000. Moreover, whereas in the South less than one per cent of the Negroes have incomes of $4,000 or more, in the North and West slightly more than two per cent have incomes within this income bracket, and one Negro in every one hundred with incomes has an income of $5,000 or more.

These income figures show clearly that the black bourgeoisie is comprised essentially of white-collar workers. The less than one per cent of Negroes with incomes between $4,000 and $5,000 and who are at the top of the pyramid of the Negro bourgeoisie, have incomes about equal to the median income of white-collar workers among whites.[12] The extremely small proportion (five in every thousand) of Negroes whose annual incomes amount to $5,000 or more includes principally physicians, dentists, lawyers, entertainers, and businessmen. The relatively large incomes of the Negroes in the professions are due partly to their business activities. A study made some years ago showed that 32 per cent of the Negro physicians and 13.5 per cent of the Negro dentists were engaged in business activities.[13] In this same income bracket ($5,000 or more), there are a few college professors, public school principals, and persons employed in the federal, state and municipal governments. The businessmen with incomes of $5,000 or more are to be found in the occupational group designated as managers, proprietors, and officials. Some of these businessmen include Negroes who have been successful in reaching the top in the rackets in the United States. In Chicago, for example, where the "policy" racket is a big business, this business was until recently "organized as a cartel in a syndicate of fifteen men including twelve Negroes."[14] The role of these businessmen in the life of the black bourgeoisie will be discussed later. We shall turn our attention to legitimate Negro business as a source of income for the black bourgeoisie.

## 3. Negro Business

Negro businesses are those enterprises which are owned and operated by Negroes.[15] These business enterprises come within the definition of small businesses; in fact, they fall within the lowest category of small businesses.[16] When the first study was made of Negro business in 1898, it was found that the average capital investment for the 1,906 businesses giving information amounted to onlyp $4,600.[17] When the latest study of Negro businesses was made in 1944, it was revealed that the average volume of business of the 3,866 Negro businesses in twelve cities was only $3,260.[18] The vast majority (90.5 per cent) of these businesses were retail stores (42.5 per cent) and service establishments (48 per cent). Although Negro businesses are operated primarily for Negroes, the total volume of sales of food stores, according to the

United States Census of Business in 1939, was only $24,-037,000, or less than two dollars for each Negro in the United States. The food stores constituted 37 per cent of the retail stores owned and operated by Negroes. Next in importance to food stores were "eating places," which together with "drinking places" comprised over 40 per cent of the retail stores. The remainder of the retail stores include filling stations, drug stores, liquor stores, second-hand stores, hardware stores, and a variety of small stores.

In 1939 there were nearly 30,000 retail stores owned and operated by Negroes, with total sales amounting to about 71.5 million dollars. According to the 1944 study of Negro business, 80 per cent of all Negro businesses were operated by their owners. As one may see from Table III, about 70 per cent of these stores were located in the southern states. Although only 27 per cent of these retail stores were in the North, their sales amounted to nearly 40 per cent of the total sales of all retail stores and the payrolls in the North accounted for 50 per cent of the total. In fact, three northern states—New York, Illinois and Ohio—accounted for 25 per cent of the total payrolls of Negro stores in the United States. Moreover, nearly 40 per cent of employees were in the stores in the North.

As we have seen above, nearly a half of Negro businesses are what we called service establishments. These businesses have grown up to serve the needs of Negroes, principally because of the refusal on the part of white establishments to provide personal services for Negroes.[19] Therefore, the majority (over 80 per cent) of these businesses consist of beauty shops, barber shops, cleaning and pressing places, undertakers, and shoe repair shops. The remainder of the businesses in this group are concerned with automobile repair and services, and with various other types of repair services.

One may get a notion of the nature of Negro business in the North by considering first the situation in Chicago.[20] During the fifteen years prior to the mass migrations from the South, the number of Negro businesses reached 500. The majority of these enterprises were in the service field, with barber shops and moving and storage establishments forming the majority of the enterprises. It was the mass migrations from the South during

### Table III—Number of Negro Owned Retail Stores, Sales, Personnel, Payroll and Stocks According to Geographic Divisions in 1939*

*EMPLOYEES*

| Geographic Division | Number of Stores | Sales (000) | Full Time | Part Time | Payroll | Stocks on Hand End of Year, at Cost |
|---|---|---|---|---|---|---|
| North | 8,272 | $29,028 | 4,106 | 1,319 | $2,727,000 | $1,326,000 |
| South | 20,825 | 39,364 | 5,756 | 2,014 | 2,344,000 | 1,543,000 |
| West | 730 | 3,074 | 358 | 225 | 305,000 | 173,000 |
| Total | 29,827 | $71,466 | 10,220 | 3,558 | $5,386,000 | $3,042,000 |

* U. S. Department of Commerce. Bureau of the Census, August 29, 1941, p. 10.

and following World War I that created the Negro market in Chicago which Negro businesses sprang up to serve. Conspicuous among the Negro businesses were the two banks and four insurance companies. During the Depression the two Negro banks failed and many of the larger business establishments were wiped out. At the same time the smaller businesses increased in number because unemployed Negroes with small savings opened small stores as a means of securing a living. In 1938 there were about 2,600 Negro businesses in Chicago. Of the ten most numerous establishments there were 287 beauty parlors, 257 groceries, 207 barber shops, 163 tailors, cleaners, and pressers, and 145 restaurants. The remaining five most numerous types of business—coal and wood dealers, taverns, undertakers, shoe repairing and dressmaking—were represented by less than 100 establishments. There were 2,800 white businesses which received more than nine-tenths of the money spent by Negroes.

The situation of Negro business enterprises in the Harlem Negro community in New York City was similar to that in Chicago.[21] A survey of 52 of the 78 census tracts in the Harlem area, or those in which one per cent or more of the total population was Negro, showed that Negroes conducted 1,928 or 18.6 per cent of the 10,319 businesses. The main type of businesses engaged in by Negroes differed considerably from the chief businesses in which whites were engaged. More than a third (36.5 per cent) of the Negro businesses provided personal services, such as barber shops, beauty parlors, and cleaning and pressing shops. On the other hand, 36.3 per cent of the businesses conducted by whites as compared with 18.4 per cent of the Negro businesses provided for the basic needs of the Negro community. These businesses included grocery stores, meat markets, bakeries, coal and ice companies, restaurants, and clothing, department and furniture stores. Moreover, a closer inspection of the types of businesses in this general class shows that the majority of Negro businesses providing the basic needs of Harlem were restaurants.

We turn now to the Negro banks, newspapers and life insurance companies, which are regarded as the major achievements of Negroes in the field of business. According to the 1951 report of the United States Department of Commerce, there were fourteen banks owned and operated by Negroes with total assets amounting to $32 million, and total deposits being $29 million.[22] All of these banks were located in the South with the exception of one in Philadelphia, another in Washington, D. C., and a third in Kansas City, Kansas. According to the study made in 1944, these banks employed from three persons in the smallest banks to fifteen persons in the largest institutions.[23] In connection with the banks there should be mentioned the financial operations of the twenty-five savings and loan associations owned and operated by Negroes, which had total assets amounting to $16 million in 1949.[24] Only passing attention need be given to consumers co-operatives here, since co-operatives did not develop among Negroes until the thirties and only two of the eleven co-operatives of any importance do an annual business of over $10,000.[25]

According to the most recent reports there are in the United States 169 Negro newspapers, 85 of which are published in the South, 66 in the North and 18 in the West.[26] All of these newspapers are weeklies with the exception of five which appear semi-weekly and two dailies. Although only a third of the Negro population is in the North, the 66 newspapers published there have 56 per cent of the total circulation of Negro newspapers. Five of the leading newspapers have nearly half of the total circulation of Negro newspapers, which is more than 2,000,000 a week. Four of the newspapers with the largest circulation are in the North and one in the South.[27] Although it is difficult to get information on the amount of capital investment represented in Negro newspapers, reliable estimates indicate that their total valuation is close to $10 million.[28] It has also been estimated that Negro newspapers provide full-time or part-time employment for about 6,000 persons.

We come finally to the Negro insurance companies, which are the largest business enterprises owned and operated by Negroes. In 1945 there were forty-four member companies in the National Negro Insurance Association.[29] The member companies had been operating on an average of twenty-four years and were classified as follows: thirty were legal reserve companies; eight assessment and mutual aid companies; five burial insurance companies; and one fraternal organization. These forty-four companies had a total of over 4,000,000 policies in force, of which 232,441 were ordinary policies, 3,860,890 industrial (health and accident), and the remainder unspecified. The median average size of the ordinary policies of the 20 companies for which information was available was $690; while the median size of the industrial policies of 41 companies was $140. The 44 companies had a total income of $42 million in 1945 and disbursements amounted to over $30 million, nearly one-half of which was paid to the employees in the 40 companies which reported on this phase of their operations. With the exception of cosmetic manufacturers which employ on the average of 37 persons, and taxi-cab companies 29 persons, the insurance companies employ a higher number of employees (24.4 persons on the average in their branch offices) than other Negro businesses.

Having given an account of the economic basis of the black bourgeoisie, we shall direct attention in the next chapter to the manner in which the mind and outlook of this class in the Negro population have been shaped principally by educational institutions.

# Chapter III

## Education of the Black Bourgeoisie

FROM ITS INCEPTION the education of the Negro was shaped by bourgeois ideals. The northern missionaries, who followed in the wake of the Union armies as they overran the South, established schools which taught the Yankee virtues of industry and thrift. Moreover, since practically all of these schools were supported by Protestant church organizations in the North, they sought to inculcate in their students the current ideals of Puritan morality. When the triumphant industrial capitalism of the North assumed the support of Negro education in the South, bourgeois ideals were given greater support. Over the years. Negro schools, the so-called "industrial" schools as well as the institutions of higher education, both public and private, have placed increasing emphasis upon professional and business education. It has been chiefly in these segregated schools in the South that the black bourgeoisie has received its education, despite the fact that a constantly increasing number of Negro students have attended northern schools in recent years.

### 1. Northern Missionaries Follow the Union Armies

As the Union armies advanced into the South, they were faced with the problem of caring for the slaves who fled from the plantations and sought a refuge in the army camps. This problem appeared first when a Union army under General Butler occupied Fortress Monroe, Virginia.[1] When slaves in the surrounding area learned that three Negro slaves, who had escaped from their masters and had entered the federal lines, were held as "contrabands," they flocked in large numbers to the Union army.[2] The men were put to work, food and shelter were provided for all the refugees, and the first day school in the South for Negroes was established by the American Missionary

Association. The first teacher of this school was a free "woman of colour" from the North who had been educated in England.

Then, as the Union armies pushed farther south and the problem of the Negro refugees became more acute, an appeal was sent out by General Sherman to philanthropic people of the North for aid for the poverty-stricken and illiterate refugees. In response to this appeal Freedmen's Aid Societies were formed in Boston, New York, and Philadelphia. A representative of the Societies, Edward L. Pierce, sailed in March, 1863, from New York with about forty-five men and fifteen women who were said to constitute "the first missionary expedition to propagate industry, religion, and education among the contrabands at Hilton Head (South Carolina), as well as encourage agriculture and like useful measures."[3] Thus began the invasion of the South by the missionaries and the much-maligned New England "schoolmarms" whose passion for humanity and idealism caused them to devote their lives to the regeneration of the emancipated blacks.

The response of the Freedmen to the idealism and devotion of these missionaries has been vividly described by Bond:

The missionary teachers from New England, fresh from the then-recent victories of Horace Mann and Henry Barnard in the battle for a free public school, encouraged the freedmen in their conviction. At no time or place in America has there been exemplified so pathetic a faith in education as the lever of racial progress. Grown men studied their alphabets in the fields, holding the "blue-back speller" with one hand while they guided the plow with the other. Mothers tramped scores of miles to towns where they could place their children in school. Pine torches illumined the dirt-floored cabins where men, women, and children studied until far into the night. No mass movement has been more in the American tradition than the urge which drove Negroes toward education soon after the Civil War.[4]

It was soon found necessary to unify the work of missionaries and the sporadic efforts of army chaplains who were interested in the welfare of the emancipated slaves. As a result, the "Bureau for Freedmen, Refugees and Abandoned Lands" was created by an act of the Congress of the United States. Although the Freedmen's Bureau, as it was known, was concerned with the general economic and social welfare of the Negro, the major part of its effort was concentrated on the education of the Negro. Despite the opposition of the southern whites, the Bureau succeeded in the five years of its operation in establishing more than 4,000 schools, in which more than 9,000 teachers gave instruction to nearly 250,000 Negro pupils.[5] The Bureau expended over $3,500,000, which was supplemented by over $1,500,000 from philanthropic societies and at least $1,000,000 in gifts and fees from the Negroes themselves.

Because of the need for Negro teachers the Bureau had to establish institutions of higher education. Consequently, within three years after the abolition of slavery, there were fourteen institutions providing teacher training and higher education in the South.[6] Among the institutions established by the Bureau were Atlanta University, Fisk University, and Howard University, which have been the chief institutions devoted to the higher education of the Negro. The work of the Bureau in establishing institutions of higher education for Negroes was supplemented by the various religious organizations. At first this work was carried on through the American Missionary Association, which established more than twelve secondary schools and colleges. But the various religious denominations preferred to assume responsibility for their own schools. The Baptists, Methodists, Presbyterians and Episcopalians established about twenty secondary schools and colleges. Later the independent Negro religious denominations established at least a half dozen colleges. Although the majority of the schools established by the Bureau and religious organizations were called "colleges" and "universities," most of their instruction did not go beyond a secondary level and only one institution, Howard University, ever became (with the support of the federal government) a real university with the various professional schools.

The establishment of Hampton Institute and Tuskegee Institute requires special attention because of their special role in the education of the Negro. Although Hampton was founded by the American Missionary Association, it developed its unique character under General Samuel Chapman Armstrong. Armstrong's educational program for the Negro was based upon his observations of the work of the Labor School at Hilo, Hawaii. He wanted to create "moral as well as mental strength" in the Negro students and, while making them "first-rate mechanical laborers," he wanted to make them "first-rate men and women." Hampton's most distinguished graduate, Booker T. Washington, who was invited to establish a normal school in Tuskegee, Alabama, established Tuskegee Institute, an institution which was based upon the ideas which he had acquired at Hampton Institute, and became famous throughout the world. The development of land-grant colleges for Negroes, which was made possible by an act of the United States Congress providing for the maintenance of an agricultural and mechanical college in each state of the Union, is a part of the history of the founding of industrial and agricultural schools for Negroes.

The program of industrial education for the Negro gave rise to a controversy in the eighteen nineties, which involved the entire question of the future status of the Negro in American society. This controversy arose at a time when the North had lost much of its idealism about the rights of the Negro as a human being and the missionaries who represented this idealism were dead or disregarded. The support of education for the Negro in the South was becoming the special concern of northern industrialists.

## 2. Capitalism and Philanthropy

Scarcely two years after the abolition of slavery, philanthropic foundations in the North began to support Negro education in the South. The Peabody Fund, which was established in 1867 through a gift of $1,000,000 by George Peabody, a banker, aided in the setting up of common schools for Negroes. The trustees of the Fund were not in favor of racial equality since they stipulated in 1871, when white and colored teachers were receiving the same salaries, that Negro schools should receive only two-thirds the allotment made to white schools. Moreover, the trustees of the Fund opposed the Civil Rights Bill pending in Congress in 1873 and gave $800 to Fisk University in 1869 in preference to Berea College where Negroes and whites were educated together. When the Peabody Fund was dissolved in 1914, its assets were turned over to the John F. Slater Fund.[7] The Slater Fund was established through a gift of $1,000,000 by John F. Slater, a merchant of Norwich, Connecticut.[8] The original purpose of the Fund was to aid institutions of higher education and vocational work in public schools, but because of the influence of Booker T. Washington, the Fund changed its emphasis to industrial education. Later, in 1910, this Fund began to support teacher-training for the graduates of the inferior rural schools for Negroes and thereby circumvented the current opposition of southern whites to secondary education for Negroes.

The establishment of these foundations for the support of Negro education in the South was only the beginning of the philanthropy of northern capitalists in this area. In 1905, a wealthy Quaker woman in Philadelphia established the Jeanes Fund with a gift of $200,000 to aid "little county schools" for Negroes. Five years later the Phelps-Stokes Fund was established for the improvement of Negro education. Before this Fund was set up, the General Education Board, which was established in 1903 by John D. Rockefeller, began to aid Negro education in the South.[9] By 1914 the General Education Board had contributed $700,000 to Negro schools. Then, even before the Julius Rosenwald Fund was established in 1917, Rosenwald, one of the principal stockholders in the Sears-Roebuck mail order establishment in Chicago, had become interested through the influence of Booker T. Washington in Negro education in the South. After the Rosenwald Fund was established it aided more than 5,000 Negro rural schools.[10] The contributions of these various foundations provide only an inadequate measure of the contributions of northern capitalists to the education of the Negro in the South. And what is more important, the figures cited provide no insight into the manner in which northern philanthropy has influenced the orientation of the educated Negro towards his position in American life.

During the last decade of the nineteenth century, when Booker T. Washington became not only the proponent of the "industrial education" for the Negro, the disfranchisement of the Negro was being achieved through law, public education for Negro children was becoming a mere mockery of education, and a legalized system of racial segregation was restricting the Negro worker to common labor and domestic service. Booker T. Washington's formula for the solution of the race problem, which he announced in his famous speech at the Atlanta Exposition in 1895, "In all things that are purely social we can be as separate as the fingers, yet one as the hand in all things essential to mutual progress,"[11] was regarded by the South as the Negro's acceptance of his subordination in American life. Northern whites welcomed the speech as an indication of the cessation of racial conflict, which had been an obstacle to their investments in the South. Moreover, northern industrialists regarded Washington's espousal of industrial education for the Negro as a logical program for the training of black industrial workers for a South that was becoming industrialized.[12] Therefore, northern industrialists accepted Washington as the spokesman of Negroes and as the arbiter in the distribution of funds for Negro education.

Washington's leadership and his educational program

were attacked by W. E. B. DuBois who had already gained distinction for his sociological studies of the Negro at Atlanta University. DuBois did not object to the training of Negroes for industry, but he recognized that Washington's program of industrial education, in the light of his formula for the solution of the race problem, involved the entire question of the Negro's status in American life. As he wrote:

> I would not deny, or for a moment seem to deny, the paramount necessity of teaching the Negro to work, and to work steadily and skillfully; or seem to depreciate in the slightest degree the important part industrial schools must play in the accomplishment of these ends, but I *do* say, and insist upon it, that it is industrialism drunk with its vision of success, to imagine that its own work can be accomplished without providing for the training of broadly cultured men and women to teach its own teachers, and to teach the teachers of the public schools.[13]

According to DuBois:

> The Negro race, like all races, is going to be saved by its exceptional men. The problem of education, then, among Negroes must first of all deal with the Talented Tenth; it is the problem of developing the Best of this race that they may guide the Mass away from the contamination and death of the Worst, in their own and other races. Now the training of men is a difficult and intricate task. Its technique is a matter for educational experts, but its object is for the vision of seers. If we make money the object of man-training, we shall develop money-makers but not necessarily men; if we make technical skill the object of education, we may possess artisans but not, in nature, men.[14]

The northern capitalists who were giving their support to Negro education in the South were not interested in making "men." The southern whites were opposed for other reasons to the development of a truly educated leadership among Negroes. DuBois had only the backing of a relatively small number of educated Negroes, especially in the North, and the vanishing remnant of northern whites who held to the idealism of the abolitionists and missionaries who had gone into the South. As a result, the schools offering "industrial education" became the recipient of millions of dollars which individual northern capitalists and foundations gave to Negro education. The schools which were devoted to "higher" education began to die when they could no longer subsist on the pittance that was offered by the charity of a few northern white idealists.

As DuBois had foreseen, the program of "industrial education" for Negroes involved the entire status of the Negro in the South. It meant that Negroes would no longer demand the right to vote or the same public education as whites, nor would they protest against lynchings and segregation. Negro leaders who protested against these denials of democratic and human rights were regarded as radicals and were often forced to leave the South. Atlanta University, where DuBois had inaugurated his sociological studies of the Negro, gradually lost the support of northern philanthropy, and he left the University to join the National Association for the Advancement of Colored People in order to free the institution from the embarrassment of his presence. At the same time, any mere pretense of an educational institution which claimed to give "industrial" education was certain to receive the support of northern philanthropists. Industrial education often became, in the American parlance, a "racket." But, of course, the schools of so-called "industrial" education were supposed to instill in their students a spirit of humility and an acceptance of their inferior status. Moreover, no teacher in a school of industrial education could mention the existence of labor unions. The emphasis of this education was supposed to be on the "heart and the hand" rather than the head because southern white people did not want the Negro's head to be educated.[15]

Industrial education for the Negro never achieved its avowed aim of training Negroes to be industrial workers. It appears from Washington's speeches that in advocating industrial education, he often confused the skills required in the traditional handicrafts and the developing skills which were required by the machine age which was making its appearance in the South. For example, in his customary picturesque fashion of speaking, he made the following statement in a lecture:

Without industrial education, when the black woman washes a shirt, she washes with both hands, both feet, and her whole body. An individual with industrial education will use a machine that washes ten times as many shirts in a given time with almost no expenditure of physical force; steam, electricity, or water doing the work.[16]

The impact of modern industry in the South had manifested itself in the textile mills from which Negro workers were completely excluded. The textile mills with their low wages were regarded as specially reserved for the "poor whites" who were migrating from the rural areas. Industrial education for the Negro was restricted to the teaching of handicrafts which were rapidly being displaced by the machine. But the white workers, with the support of the white owning classes, generally opposed the teaching of mechanical skills that would enable Negroes to compete with them. Home economics and domestic science were favored subjects because they were supposed to train Negroes to become cooks for white people. Although the graduates of "industrial" schools did not become industrial workers, they did not become domestic servants. They became teachers in the inferior schools provided for Negroes in the South or they went on to schools where they could receive a broader, or a professional, education.[17] Washington had evidently become aware of this as early as the eighteen nineties in view of what he stated to the students at Tuskegee Institute during one of his famous Sunday evening talks:

I believe that the majority of students who graduate from Tuskegee should work in what is known as the "Black Belt" of the South, and I am glad that the majority of our graduates have done so thus far, and are working in one way and another for the elevation of those about them. You will hear many students, especially those in the higher classes, say that they intend to practice medicine, study law, or something else, when they graduate; but the majority after all, will be found in these fields of work that lie about in the black belt of the South, where our best talent and influence are needed.[18]

## 3. Piety, Thrift, and Respectability

The missionaries from New England who founded the first schools for Negroes in the South left the imprint of their Puritan background upon Negro education. Although by 1830 Puritanism in New England had begun to decline, it was still a dominant force in the lives of the people. For example, in 1830 employers in New England were able to oppose the reduction of the number of hours of labor to ten hours on the ground that too much leisure time would encourage vice among workers.[19] There were still restrictions upon amusements and the profanation of the Sabbath. As the result of the influx of European immigrants and the Civil War, New England and in fact the United States as a whole began to discard its prudery and puritanical morals. But the missionaries who came from New England represented the native English stock and were imbued with the Puritan tradition. As a consequence they maintained a strict surveillance over the conduct of their Negro students in order to stamp out any tendencies towards frivolous or immoral conduct.

Because of the system of social control in these missionary schools, it was not difficult to maintain an atmosphere of piety. All of the students were required to attend chapel once or twice a day. At the chapel exercises they heard the reading of the Bible, which was followed by a prayer. Generally some lesson was drawn from the Scriptures in order to show its application to their lives.

Visiting speakers who appeared at the chapel exercises were selected with a view to seeing that their talk would fit into the "spirit of the school." As a result, representatives of the Young Men's Christian Association or Young Women's Christian Association and similar organizations proved to be the most eligible speakers for such occasions. The pious teachings at the chapel exercises were reinforced in the weekly prayer meetings. The whole emphasis of these various meetings was to give the students a sentimental and moral as opposed to a rational and scientific outlook on life. Moral behavior meant that the students were not to dance, smoke, or play cards. In some schools a concession was made to the desire on the part of the students to dance by permitting them to "march" on social occasions. But a strict surveillance was maintained in order to prevent any steps that would be surreptitious dancing. In such an environment of piety it was natural that chapel services on Sunday were especially important and that the students should spend the day as quietly as possible, even refraining from light or frivolous conversation.

Many industrial schools maintained an atmosphere as pious as the colleges; and when the Negroes themselves began to assume control of their schools, they tried to maintain the same tradition of piety. At Tuskegee Institute, which was always under the control of Negroes, the tradition of piety was almost as strong as at Hampton Institute which was under white control. At the chapel exercises moral conduct, which included refraining from playing cards, was stressed by Washington, who said:

Do not play cards. Playing cards, you will insist, is no more harmful than playing dominoes or croquet; but it is a fact undeniable that playing cards leads to something more harmful than either of the games I have just mentioned. Card-playing has a history, and it is the experience of men who understand crime, who understand civilization in all its grades, that card-playing has been the source of any number of crimes. It leads to late hours, bad company, a betting proclivity, and, finally, it leads to the using of other people's money.[20]

However, for Washington, morality and religion should be mixed with worldly goods:

> We might as well settle down to the uncompromising fact that our people will grow in proportion as we teach them that the way to have the most of Jesus and in a permanent form is to mix with their religion some land, cotton, and corn, a house with two or three rooms, and a little bank account. With these interwoven with our religion, there will be a foundation for growth upon which we can build for all time.[21]

The tradition of piety in the schools founded by the missionaries continued well into the fourth decade of the present century. A Frenchman who spent some time as a professor of French in a Negro college for girls especially favored by the Rockefeller philanthropies, has written a vivid account of its pious atmosphere.[22] The first thing that struck this European observer was the fact that about 98 per cent of the students were mulattoes and not "pure" Negroes as he had expected to find. This institution, with its "missionary idea," maintained an "almost prison-like surveillance over its hand-picked students." The faculty was described as consisting principally of "righteous and strait-laced New England women." There were three categories of teachers: timid white virgins who were seeking salvation through the uplifting of the descendants of Uncle Tom, a number of radicals who dared not express their radical beliefs, and morons who compensated for their inferiority by lording over benighted Negroes. The chief aim of this college was Christianization and moral training. The academic standing of the students was determined largely by the extent to which they had developed a "religious spirit." The "religious spirit" of the students was measured by the extent to which they submitted to the requirements concerning attendance at the chapel exercises, at meetings of the Young Women's Christian Association, and at prayer meetings.

In the pious atmosphere of this missionary school, the students were found to be listless and without any desire to learn. There was some resentment among the students against the system of control, but on the whole they submittedly silently for fear of losing an opportunity to secure an education. They seemed to suffer from an unjustified fear that if they did not exhibit a "spirit of cheerful gratitude" towards the white northerners, they would be expelled from the school. The only concession that was made to the Negro's culture was that the students were required to sing Spirituals for the white visitors. But though the school was saturated with religious feeling, the required religious activities were designed to wean them from the religious emotionalism of the Negro. The graduates of this college would teach, as this European rightly observes, "what little they knew" to real "Negroes whom they did not know."

In the pious environment of the colleges the students were taught to be industrious and thrifty, wasting neither time nor money. The regimen and discipline of these colleges were designed to teach these ideals. Moreover, because of the close association of teachers and students, the students learned by the example set by their teachers as well as by precept. Also, the literary training given by these schools was represented in the habits, enjoyments, and ideals of their teachers. In the industrial schools the ideal of thrift was tied up with labor. Booker T. Washington had regarded the teaching of "the dignity of labor" to be one of the primary tasks of industrial education. In his Atlanta speech, he had stated:

> Our greatest danger is that in the great leap from slavery to freedom we may overlook the fact that the masses of us are to live by the production of our hands, and fail to keep in mind that we shall prosper in proportion as we learn to dignify and glorify common labor, and put brains and skill in the common occupations of life.[23]

In his Sunday evening chapel talks, Washington constantly urged the students to be efficient and to dignify labor. One of these talks was concerned with the manner in which the Negro barbers had lost out in competition with whites:

During the past twenty-five or thirty years we have let some golden opportunities slip from us, and I fear we have not had enough plain talk right on these lines. If you ever have the opportunity to go into the large cities of the North, you will see some striking examples of this kind of thing. I remember the first time I went North—and it hasn't been so many years ago—it was not an uncommon thing to see the barber shops in the hands of colored men. I know colored men who could have gotten comfortably rich. You cannot find today a first-class barber shop in New York or Boston in the hands of a colored man. Something is wrong. That opportunity is gone. Coming home, in Montgomery, Memphis, or New Orleans, you will find that the barber shops are gradually slipping from the hands of the colored men, and they are going back on dark streets and opening little holes. These opportunities have slipped from us largely because we have not learned to dignify labor. The colored man puts a little dirty chair and a pair of razors into a dirtier-looking hole, while the white man opens up his shop in connection with some fashionable hotel, fits it up in fine style with carpets, fine mirrors, etc., and calls that a Tonsorial Parlor. The proprietor sits up at his desk, keeps his books, and takes the cash. Thus he transforms what we call a drudgery into a paying business.[24]

To dignify labor and make it more efficient were not, according to Washington, ends in themselves. They are the means to become business enterpreneurs and share in the profits of business:

We must not only teach the Negro to improve the methods of what are now classed as the lower forms of labor, but the Negro must be put in a position, by the use of intelligence and skill, to take his part in the higher forms of labor, up in the region where the profits appear.[25]

From the head of Tuskegee Institute, the students learned that: "A man never begins to have self-respect until he owns a home."[26] And that:

Art and music to people who live in rented houses and with no bank account are not the most important subjects to which attention can be given. Such education creates wants without a corresponding ability to supply these increased wants.[27]

There was one point on which the proponents of industrial education and higher education were agreed: the Negro student should strive to be respectable. As we have seen, DuBois had said that "the Best of the race" should "guide the mass away from the Worst." And Booker T. Washington, who always counseled his students against the shiftlessness and rude behavior of Negroes, told them in one Sunday evening talk:

There is a beauty, a transformation, as it were, a regeneration, that takes place in the physical make-up of a young man or young woman who gets into the habit of living on the high side of life rather than on the lower side.[28]

Negro students were supposed to be differentiated in their morals as well as in their manners from the Negro masses. For that reason they were not to indulge in the religious emotionalism of the black masses. In some cases the core of the student bodies of the schools founded by the missionaries consisted of the children of Negroes, predominantly mulattoes, who were free before the Civil War.[29] It was not difficult to get the children of this favored group, which was differentiated from the ex-slaves by education and general culture, to conform to the standards of respectability. But where the schools drew their student bodies more largely from the masses of freedmen, a strict discipline was necessary in order to inculcate and maintain standards of respectability. First, students were taught to speak English correctly and thus avoid the ungrammatical speech and dialect of the Negro masses. They were expected to be courteous, speak softly and never exhibit the spontaneous boisterousness of ordinary Negroes. When they walked down the street, people should be able to say, "There goes a X college girl or boy."

The young men, but more especially the young women, were to live chaste lives. To be detected in immoral sex behavior, especially if the guilty person was a woman, meant expulsion from the school. It was only "common" Negroes who engaged in premarital and unconventional sex relations. The graduates of these schools were to go forth and become the heads of conventional families. Was this not the best proof of respectability in the eyes of the white man, who had constantly argued that the Negro's "savage instincts" prevented him from conforming to puritanical standards of sex behavior?

## 4. From the Making of Men to the Making of Money-Makers

The mass migration of Negroes from the South during and following the first World War affected the education of the Negro as it did other phases of his life. When hundreds of thousands of Negroes who had migrated to northern cities gained access to the same education as whites, the controversy concerning the relative merits of industrial education and higher education lost its significance. In the South, where industrialization was making rapid progress, school boards began to show a willingness to have the less expensive classical courses, such as Latin, taught in Negro high schools while instituting technical and vocational courses in white high schools.[30] There was also a change in the attitudes of southern whites toward college education for Negroes, but Negro institutions of higher education continued to receive only a small fraction of the State appropriation for higher education.[31]

The philanthropic foundations in the North responded quickly to the changing situation and began to give millions of dollars to the higher education of Negroes.[32] In 1930 the American Missionary Association and the Methodist Church (North) which had maintained colleges for Negroes in New Orleans, joined with the Julius Rosenwald Fund and the General Education Board in consolidating their Negro colleges and projected Dillard University. According to the arrangement, the two church organizations contributed $1,000,000, the two foundations $750,000, and the citizens of New Orleans, with the co-operation of the Chamber of Commerce, $250,000 for the site of the new university. In 1929 the General Education board gave $1,500,000 towards new buildings and $1,-700,000 towards the endowment of a university system based upon the existing five Negro colleges which were carrying on a precarious existence. The Atlanta University system took its name from the old Atlanta University which had engaged in a valiant but losing struggle for the higher education of Negroes. In line with this new interest of northern philanthropies in the higher education of the Negro was the decision of the federal government to legalize and increase its appropriations to Howard University.[33] Since Congress made its first appropriation in 1879, Howard University had depended upon small annual grants by Congress. It was not until 1928 that Congress passed legislation legalizing regular and substantial appropriations to the University. During the following year representatives of the federal government and the Julius Rosenwald Fund met with representatives of the University to plan a program of expansion.

While these changes were occurring in the attitude of the South and the philanthropic foundations toward the higher education of the Negro, the Negro was beginning to assume greater control of his education. In 1926, the first Negro was elected president of Howard University.

The Atlanta University system was set up under a Negro president. Negro students as well as teachers were demanding that their schools be placed under Negro administrators.[34] The election of Negro administrators in Negro colleges represented to a certain extent a revolt against missionary education. But the transformation which was occurring indicated something more fundamental than a change from white to Negro administration.

The entire orientation and aim of higher education of Negroes was changing. It was natural that as the result of the revolt against missionary education, these institutions would lose much of their piety. Dancing, card playing, and smoking ceased to be deadly sins and requirements concerning chapel attendance were modified. Only in the smaller and isolated schools did the tradition of piety linger. Then there was less talk about thrift and the dignity of labor. The change which occurred at Tuskegee Institute which was devoted to industrial education for the Negro masses, is a measure of the extent of the transformation. Tuskegee Institute began to grant academic degrees and the students began to wear the academic cap and gown as was the custom in the institutions of higher education. Moreover, in all the institutions, the canons of respectability were undergoing a radical change. Respectability became less a question of morals and manners and more a matter of the external marks of a high standard of living.

As the children of the Negro masses have flooded the colleges, it was inevitable that the traditional standards of morals and manners would have to give way. These children of peasants had no particular interest in learning to speak correctly nor in cultivating the gentility of their predecessors who had come under the strict discipline of northern missionaries. Many of them, having come from a background of disorganized family life, were strangers to the traditional puritanical morality of these schools. A chance for a college education represented for them the chief means of achieving social and economic mobility. The colleges had to make concessions to their poor educational and social backgrounds.[35] But the children of the Negro masses were not primarily responsible for the change in the character of the Negro college. The outlook and aims of the colleges changed in response to the aspirations and values of the second generation of Negro college students and their Negro teachers who were imbued with middle-class values.

Unlike the missionary teachers, the present teachers have little interest in "making men," but are concerned primarily with teaching as a source of income which will enable them to maintain middle-class standards and participate in Negro "society." It appears that the majority of them have no knowledge of books nor any real love of literature. Today many of the teachers of English and literature never read a book as a source of pleasure or recreation. They go through a dull routine of teaching literature or other college subjects to listless students, many of whom cannot read.[36]

The second and third generations of Negro college students are as listless as the children of peasants. The former are interested primarily in the activities of Greek letter societies and "social" life, while the latter are concerned with gaining social acceptance by the former. Both are less concerned with the history or the understanding of the world about them than with their appearance at the next social affair. The girl with a peasant or working-class background may be irritated by her mother's inability to buy an expensive "party" dress. But what can be expected when the dean of women has instructed her to tell her mother that she must have the dress at any sacrifice? So teachers and students alike are agreed that money and conspicuous consumption are more important than knowledge or the enjoyment of books and art and music.

That the teachers are as imbued with the same middle-class values as their students is indicated by their whole style of life. Some idea of the values and style of life of the present-day Negro teacher in the Negro college may be gained from an illuminating analysis by a white teacher of the reasons why the Negro and white teachers on a Negro college campus could not talk, laugh, or relax together.[37] On this college campus the white teachers were not missionaries but were liberal white couples who had accepted positions at the college because they were interested in teaching and in breaking down racial barriers. But they found that it was impossible to associate freely with their colored colleagues because the latter had a different style of life and a different set of values.

The white couples were pacifists and were interested in co-operatives. They were enthusiastic about folk dancing and were committed to internationalism and interracialism. Although a few Negro teachers shared these interests, none of them had a pattern of life similar to that of their white colleagues. The Negro teachers had accepted their teaching positions because of the social status and economic security which the positions provided. Unlike their white colleagues, they were conservative and against pacifism and had no interest in social questions. Conversation and books had no place in their recreation, which consisted in playing cards, drinking, movies, and "parties." Their interest was in automobiles, furniture, and household appliances, the same values as the rising white middle class. Even on informal social occasions they would not sit on the floor as their white colleagues did. Their intense devotion to their Greek letter societies appeared to be their *raison d'être*. While their white colleagues were inclined to return to religion, the Negro teachers were fleeing from religion. From the standpoint of their values the Negro teachers could have found more congenial association with the prejudiced white middle class than with white liberals. In fact, in their struggle to attain American middle-class ideals, they gave the impression of being super-Americans.

The majority of the graduates of Negro colleges, including the land-grant colleges and vocational schools, have entered professional occupations.[38] The majority of present-day college students still aspire to the same field of activity. In recent years, however, Negro colleges have increasingly instituted courses in education for business. When a survey of Negro business and education for business was made nearly a decade ago, there were sixteen Negro colleges offering courses in business education, and other colleges were planning to institute such courses.[39] Only five per cent of the fathers of the students who were pursuing courses in business education were engaged in business, while the majority of their fathers were unskilled workers. Many of these students, coming from poor homes and with inadequate academic preparation, have undoubtedly seized upon business education as a means to rise to middle-class status. They have also been told that by becoming money-makers they would help the Negro to achieve economic independence in American life.

Thus it has turned out that Negro higher education has become devoted chiefly to the task of educating the black bourgeoisie. The United Negro College Fund, which was started in 1944, provides the small sum of about two million dollars for thirty-two Negro colleges.[40] This is a gesture on the part of white America, expressing its approval of middle-class education for Negroes behind the walls of segregation. Sometimes the appeal to white America is made on the sentimental grounds that the schools receiving financial support are educating the "children of slaves" who are thirsting for "knowledge" which will enable them to become "men." But the present generation of Negro college students (who are not the children but the great grand-children of slaves) do not wish to recall their past. As they ride to school in their automobiles, they prefer to think of the money which they will earn as professional and business men. For they have been taught that money will bring them justice and equality in American life, and they propose to get money.

# Chapter IV

## Power and Political Orientation

SINCE THE BLACK bourgeoisie is composed chiefly of white-collar workers and since its small business enterprises are insignificant in the American economy, the black bourgeoisie wields no political power as a class in American society. Nor does the black bourgeoisie exercise any significant power within the Negro community as an employer of labor. Its power within the Negro community stems from the fact that middle-class Negroes hold strategic positions in segregated institutions and create and propagate the ideologies current in the Negro community. In the political life of the American society the Negro political leaders, who have always had a middle-class outlook, follow an opportunistic policy. They attempt to accommodate the demands of Negroes for better economic and social conditions to their personal interests which are tied up with the political machines, which in turn are geared to the interests of the white propertied classes.

## 1. Brotherhood and Power

The most important institution which the Negro has built in the United States is the Negro church. Contrary to the claim of some students of the Negro that the Negro church was an African survival resurrected on American soil, the Negro church is a product of the American environment.[1] The form of its organization and the character of its religious services were the result of the proselytizing of Protestant missionaries, especially the Baptist and the Methodist missionaries. This does not mean that the Negro's peculiar experience in America did not contribute to the shaping of the institution.[2] The influence of the Negro's experience in the building of his church is seen in the variations in the character of the Negro church, which reflect the extent of the Negro's education and isolation in American life and his economic and social status.

The Negro church has two roots: one in the efforts of the free Negroes in the North to escape from their inferior position in white churches and assert their independence, and the other in what has been aptly called "the invisible" institution on the plantations during slavery.[3] During the last quarter of the eighteenth and beginning of the nineteenth century the free Negroes in Philadelphia and New York City organized the African Methodist Episcopal Church and the African Methodist Episcopal Zion Church.[4] After the Civil War, the Negro members of the white Methodist Episcopal Church (South) set up an independent denomination, the Colored Methodist Episcopal Church. In these three Methodist denominations there are two million members in about 12,000 congregations. During the period when these independent Methodist denominations were being organized, Negroes were also setting up Baptist churches in both northern and southern cities. There are 7,000,000 members in the 35,000 or more Baptist churches, each of which is an independent body.[5]

Although much of the religious life of the slaves was under the supervision of their masters and even shared with their masters, they were allowed some freedom. Thus the "invisible institution" of the Negro church grew up where the slaves were permitted to conduct their religious services with a Negro preacher. Under such circumstances, there was greater freedom of religious expression on the part of the slaves. After emancipation, the "invisible institution" became visible and merged with the independent Baptist and Methodist Negro organizations.

So important has been the Negro church in the life of the Negro in the South that the Negro population has been divided into two large religious communities—Baptists and Methodists. Consequently, the Negro church has provided the arena for the political struggles of a people shut out from the political life of the American community.

These political struggles have been especially important within the three large Negro Methodist churches, with their hierarchical organization. The bishops in their various episcopal districts have exercised an autocratic power over the lives of the ministers, who receive their church appointments from the bishops. Although the majority of the bishops and ministers in the Methodist churches have come up from the masses, their leaders have increasingly adopted a secular outlook toward the world and given support to the current values of black middle classes.

The Negro Baptist congregations have always attracted more than twice as many members as the Methodist churches. Lacking an organization with a centralized authority and hierarchy, the thousands of independent Baptist congregations have provided a wide field for self-assertion on the part of Negroes who desired to become leaders. The memberships of the congregations of the Baptist Church, which is even more than the Methodist Church the church of the Negro masses, range from less than 50 to as much as 10,000 Relatively few Negroes of middle-class status have become ministers of the Baptist congregations, though middle-class Negroes are represented more largely in the activities of the National Conventions of Baptist Churches. In some cities the Baptist congregations have split along color and class lines, as middle-class members of the Baptist churches have sought to dissociate themselves from the emotional religious activities of the Negro masses.

Only a relatively few Negroes have been attracted to the other religious denominations or the Catholic Church. The majority of upper-class Negroes who were free before the Civil War and their descendants were affiliated with the Protestant Episcopal Church and the Congregational Church. In Louisiana a large majority of the free mulattoes and their descendants have always been Catholics. As Negroes have moved up the social ladder within the Negro community, they have tended to desert the Baptist and Methodist churches and seek affiliation with the Episcopal, Congregational, Presbyterian and Catholic churches. On the other hand, many Negroes in the professional occupations have continued membership in the Methodist and Baptist churches because their clients are in these churches. Sometimes they may maintain two church memberships, one because of their social status and the other because of the financial advantages.

Where the Negro has had the right to vote, the Negro church has been regarded as a powerful influence in politics. When Negroes migrated to northern cities, the influence of ministers over their congregations was utilized to secure the traditional support which Negroes had given the Republican Party. When, however, during the Depression years, in the 1930's, the Negro masses shifted their support to the Democratic Party, which offered a solution to their economic problems, Negro ministers were forced to follow the changed outlook of their members in regard to political and economic problems. The important role of the Negro church was recognized in the struggle to secure the membership of Negro workers in the new unions being organized in the 1930's by the Congress of Industrial Organizations. The managers of large corporations undertook through contributions to Negro churches to persuade Negro workers not to join the unions.[6] Although they were able to influence some Negro ministers, it was through the efforts of some liberal Negro ministers that the Negro learned the role of unions in modern industry.

Next to the Negro church, the various fraternal organizations have represented the most influential associations which Negroes have built up within their segregated social life. The oldest of these secret societies is the Masonic Order, which was organized in Boston in 1775.[7] The next oldest secret society is the Odd Fellows, which was accepted by the English organization in 1843 after having been refused affiliation by the American society.[8] Before the Civil War two other Negro secret societies, the Galilean Fishermen and the Nazarites, were organized by the free Negroes. Then after Emancipation a number of secret societies were set up, including the Knights and Daughters of Tabor in 1871, and the Grand United Order of True Reformers in 1876, the independent Order of Good Samaritans in 1877, and the Colored Knights of Pythias in 1880.[9] The Good Samaritans was unique in that Negroes were admitted to the parent organization which was white, but when they became numerous they were encouraged to set up their own organization. The Colored Pythias is also of son. interest because Negroes who could pass for white became members of the white organization in order to learn the ritual. But the True Reformers is of most interest for this study because, as we have seen, this organization more than any other set up a number of business undertakings and spread the spirit of business enterprise.

Although some of the Negro fraternal orders or secret societies were founded by men of humble origin, the leadership in these organizations has generally been held by middle-class Negroes. In fact, Negro politicians have always gained power through their membership in these fraternal orders.[10] These various secret societies have undergone changes since the Negro became largely a city dweller. They have lost much of their religious character and have thereby ceased to be sacred brotherhoods, providing aid in time of sickness and death. For these benefits Negroes have turned to the more secure benefits of Negro insurance companies, which represent the greatest achievements of Negro business enterprise. Only one of the various national secret societies has increased its membership since Negroes have moved to cities during recent decades. That society is the Improved Benevolent and Protective Order of Elks of the World, which in its program and general spirit is more congenial to the changed outlook and interests of urbanized Negroes.[11]

The colored Order of Elks was founded by a Pullman porter in 1898.[12] Its right to existence was challenged by the white organization, but since the colored Elks had copyrighted the ritual, a procedure which the white organization had overlooked, the colored Order of Elks was allowed to continue its existence. The organization did not grow rapidly until the 1920's, when under the dynamic leadership of J. Finley Wilson, large numbers of Negroes in cities were attracted to the Order. The membership grew from 32,000 in 1922 to 500,000 members in 1,000 lodges in 1946. According to the 1946 report, the various lodges owned $30,000,000 in United States War Bonds and $25,000,000 in Elks Homes and other property. The phenomenal growth of this fraternal organization was due to the fact that it appealed to the new interests of the urban Negroes. There has been some appeal in its colorful parades and crack drill teams and military bands. But the more fundamental appeal has been its program including scholarships conducted by its Department of Education; the support which its department of Civil Rights has given to the struggle of the Negro for equality; and the gifts of equipment to the two Negro medical schools. Moreover, unlike the older fraternal orders this organization is secular in its outlook and offers a form of social participation and recognition for those elements among the Negro masses which seek a middle-class way of life despite their little education and small earnings.

The colored Order of Elks is in the hands of Negro men and women of middle-class status who derive a large income from their positions in the organization. Because of the predominantly working-class membership of the Order of Elks a middle-class Negro, if he is a doctor or college professor, will generally "explain" his membership in the Elks on the grounds that it is necessary for his profession, or that he can render "service." Nevertheless, the Order of Elks is a means of power and income for middle-class Negroes, and there is an intense struggle for the offices in the organization. Since the organization provides a good means of influencing Negro voters, both white and Negro politicians regard it as a strategic approach to the Negro community. Although many of the middle-class leaders of the Elks have been connected with Republican Party organizations, they have been forced to take into consideration the fact that the interests of the Negro masses have been with the liberal program of the Democratic Party. The leaders of the fraternal organization provides a classic example of the manner in which middle-class Negro leaders undertake to reconcile their personal interests with those of the Negro masses who are responsible for their power in the Negro community.

It is in the Greek letter fraternities that the so-called intellectual members of the black bourgeoisie often gain recognition and power. Negro Greek letter societies arose as the result of the refusal of white Greek letter societies to admit colored people. The first of these societies, Sigma Pi Phi (which has come to be known simply as the Boulé) was organized in Philadelphia in 1904, when there were relatively few Negro college graduates and professional people scattered about the country.[13] Although the original aim of this society was to bring together the "aristocracy of talent," it has become one of the main expressions of social snobbishness on the part of the black bourgeoisie. Two years after this society was organized, the first Negro Greek letter society for college students was set up at Cornell University.[14] A number of chapters of this fraternity were soon set up in Negro and white colleges. Then after a few years, Greek letter societies for both men and women were organized with chapters in the various Negro colleges of the South.[15]

These Greek letter societies are especially important in molding the outlook of the black bourgeoisie. In the Negro colleges, membership in these organizations indicates that the student has escaped from his working-class background and achieved middle-class status. In their social activities these societies foster all the middle-class values, especially conspicuous consumption. Moreover, they tend to divert the students from a serious interest in education. The leadership and control of these college fraternities are actually in the hands of adult men and women who use the organizations as a source of income. In their enthusiasm for their fraternities and sororities, these adult leaders give the impression that they have never grown up. The fraternities represent very often the widest social and intellectual orientation of the leaders as well as their deepest loyalties. One college professor, who was a "great fraternity man," stated that the three things which he loved most were his God, his wife and his fraternity. All of the fraternities and sororities attempt to justify their existence on the grounds that they render service to the Negro masses. One Greek letter sorority has established health projects for Negroes in the South and another maintained for a while a lobby in Washington to watch federal legislation affecting Negroes. But the real spirit of these societies is best represented by the Greek letter fraternity which conducts a campaign for "Better and Bigger Negro Business."

## 2. "Service" and the Intelligentsia

The activities of the Greek letter societies represent only a small part of the activities of the Negro intelligentsia influencing the thought and aspirations of the Negro. In their roles of teachers, social workers, doctors, and leaders of organizations concerned with the advancement of Negroes, the intelligentsia exercise a powerful influence on the ideologies and values of Negroes. Already we have seen something of the outlook of the present generation of teachers in Negro schools. Here we shall consider in more detail their influence as well as that of other representatives of the Negro intelligentsia in the Negro community.

Negro educational institutions, unlike the Negro church, did not grow out of the traditional culture of the Negro folk. The schools maintained by the free Negroes before the Civil War were the result of the assimilation of European culture, while the schools built by the Negro religious organizations were imitations of culture patterns alien to the Negro's way of life. The Negro colleges and schools that were established by northern white missionaries represented an entirely alien conception of life and culture from the standpoint of the social heritage of the

Negro masses. While the first generation of Negro teachers who gradually replaced the early white teachers enjoyed considerable prestige among the Negro masses, they too were in a sense representatives of the white man's way of life—and what is important for our discussion at this point is the fact that they were dependent upon the whites who had provided their education. Thus from the beginning, the Negro intelligentsia, or what DuBois called the "Talented Tenth," was created by philanthropic foundations supported by northern industrialists.

Scarcely two years after the close of the Civil War, the Peabody Fund was established to aid in the education of Negro teachers. The trustees of this Fund opposed the mixed schools for whites and Negroes and opposed the Civil Rights Bill before the United States Congress which was designed to guarantee equal educational facilities and other civil rights for Negroes.[16] Negro teachers who were beneficiaries of the Fund were expected to conform to the racial policy of this foundation. From the time when this philanthropic foundation was created until the present, the Negro intellectual has been forced to shape not only his philosophy of racial adjustment but his general social philosophy according to the social philosophy of the northern philanthropic foundations. It has not been necessary, of course, for the foundations to make explicit demands upon the Negro teacher or intellectual. The Negro teacher or intellectual realized that if he were to secure employment, he must indicate that his ideas of racial adjustment conformed to the social philosophy of the foundations. This was especially true in the case of the beneficiaries of the Rosenwald Fund, which was set up as the result of the influence of Booker T. Washington. This foundation undertook to subsidize aspiring Negroes in the fields of art, literature, and science as well as in the teaching profession. It was hostile to any Negro who showed independence in his thinking in regard to racial and economic problems. When leaders like DuBois and a few others had gained sufficient prestige and security in their professions as not to be crushed by its power, the Fund was willing to grant them aid and claim them as allies.

The segregated schools in which Negro teachers had to find employment were generally under the autocratic control of Negroes chosen by the whites who gave financial support to the schools, or the white educational authorities in charge of the schools in the South. The relation of the Negro heads of schools and of other segregated institutions depending upon white support to the Negro educated class amounted to what is known in the field of colonial administration as a system of "indirect rule." Often when Negro teachers became restive under this system of control, they were warned that they could not find employment outside of Negro schools. In fact, some Negro teachers were placed upon a "blacklist," indicating that they were not fit to teach in Negro schools because they did not have the "right" philosophy of racial adjustment. A teacher could be placed upon the "blacklist" by merely refusing to submit to insults by southern whites. Under such a system of tutelage the Negro teacher has been able to teach students only an opportunistic philosophy with reference to the race problem or the economic problems facing the country.

A relatively large proportion of educated Negroes have found employment in the field of social work. In this field of employment, as in the teaching field, the Negro intellectual has not been able to engage in independent thinking. Social welfare among Negroes has been supported by white philanthropy, and Negro workers in social welfare agencies have supported, on the whole, the ideas of their white benefactors concerning racial and economic questions. The leading organization in the field of social work devoted to the Negro has been the National Urban League. This organization, which grew out of several committees of philanthropic whites interested in the welfare of the Negro in northern cities, came into existence in 1911.[17] From its beginning the Urban League emphasized the interracial character of its program. The staff of the Urban League was composed of Negroes, with a sociologist as its executive secretary, while wealthy whites including John D. Rockefeller, Jr., Julius Rosenwald, and Mrs. William H. Baldwin were among its main financial supporters. Soon after its organization, the League established branches in the industrial centers of the North. Consequently, during the first World War, the League became the most important agency in screening the raw southern Negro recruits to northern industry and assisted in finding them homes and in making available to them the resources of the social welfare agencies.

It was inevitable that the League should become involved in the problem of the relation of the Negro workers to the labor unions. In 1919, at its annual meeting in Detroit, the National Urban League declared itself in favor of collective bargaining and stated that the Negro worker "should begin to think more and more in the terms of the labor movement."[18] Then again in 1933, when President Roosevelt's New Deal program was inaugurated, the League reiterated its belief in collective bargaining.[19] These liberal pronouncements on the part of the National Office did not have any effect on the policies followed by the local Leagues. The local Leagues shaped their policies according to the demands of the white employers whose financial support made their existence possible. In a number of cities the local Leagues utilized their relations with Negroes to engage in strike breaking, or they went into plants to discourage Negroes from organizing.[20] The local Leagues were even careful about supporting Negroes in the organization of separate unions, as in the case of the Pullman porters. When Eugene K. Jones, the executive secretary of the National Urban League announced his endorsement of the Pullman Porters Union during a financial drive in 1926, the Pullman Company, which made contributions to the Chicago Urban League, demanded to know if Mr. Jones was speaking for the Urban League or only personally.[21] Upon receiving the reply that the National Urban League

handled national questions and did not control the policies of the local Leagues, the Pullman Company continued to contribute to the Chicago Urban League.

However, the National Urban League has also followed an opportunistic policy in regard to the labor
movement. It was slow in giving its endorsement of the
organization of the Congress of Industrial Organizations.[22]
Its support of movements to unionize Negro workers has
advanced only as its white supporters have allowed it
to advance. The National Urban League does not have
the support of the Negro masses. It is an organization composed of Negro professional and white-collar workers
depending upon white philanthropy. The leaders in the
National Urban League regard themselves as essentially
social welfare workers. Even when the League organized
the so-called "Workers Councils" during the 1930's, when
Negro workers were making increasing demands for organization, they selected for membership in the Councils
middle-class Negroes who had little knowledge of Negro
workers or sympathy with their aspirations.[23]

The National Association for the Advancement of Colored People, which was also a form of interracial co-
operation for the improvement of the Negro, was organized two years before the National Urban League. It
differed from the League in that it represented a co-
operative effort on the part of the so-called "militant"
Negroes, who were opposed to the program of Booker
T. Washington, and distinguished white leaders of public
opinion who were opposed to the segregation and disfranchisement of the Negro.[24] W. E. B. DuBois, who
became the editor of *The Crisis,* the official organ of the
National Association for the Advancement of Colored
People, was the leader of the "militant" Negroes, and
Oswald Garrison Villard, the grandson of the great abolitionist, William Lloyd Garrison, wrote the call for the
conference at which the National Association for the
Advancement of Colored People was organized. When
the association was organized in 1909, its program included the following goals:

Abolition of Enforced Segregation;
Equal Educatoinal Advantages for Colored and White;
Enfranchisement for the Negro;
Enforcement of the Fourteenth and Fifteenth Amendments of the United States Constitution.

The program "was denounced by nearly every white man who gave to Negro institutions."[25] Moreover, many Negroes, especially those who were associated with institutions supported by white philanthropists, "thought" that this program was too radical, and there was pressure from both whites and Negroes to modify the program.

Negroes who became identified with the National Association for the Advancement of Colored People were known as "radical" and thus radicalism came to be associated with "racial radicalism" or the belief in the equality of Negroes and whites in American society. "Racial radicalism" had nothing to do with "radicalism" in the broader meaning of the term. It is true, however, that in the fight for equality in American society, the Association insisted upon the equality of Negroes in labor unions. As the result of the mass migrations of Negroes to northern cities during and following the first World War, membership in the Association grew rapidly. Among its middle-class leaders there were many who realized that the traditional attitude of Negro leaders toward labor was opposed to the interest of the Negro masses. Consequently, they were active in having the NAACP send to the American Federation of Labor a demand that it remove its racial bars in order that Negro workers might not be used as "scabs" and that white and black workers unite in the common struggle against the exploitation of labor.[26] Although the NAACP presented concrete proposals to bring about an end to racial discrimination in the unions, this effort on the part of middle-class leaders did not affect the position of Negro workers in the labor movement. When the Congress of Industrial Organizations began to organize Negro workers, the NAACP was divided in its attitude toward the CIO. The liberal members were favorable to the participation of Negro workers in the organization, while the conservative members were opposed on the ground that the organization was radical.[27]

Despite the failure of the NAACP to influence the position of the Negro workers in the labor unions, it has, nevertheless, helped to win significant victories for the Negro in his struggle for equal citizenship. The NAACP has won these battles through court decisions in favor of the Negro, a procedure which involved the tremendous expense of carrying cases of Negroes' rights to the United States Supreme Court where the questions involved were adjudicated on constitutional grounds. During these legal battles, the Association has won the right of the Negro voter to participate in the primary elections of the Democratic Party in the South,[28] the right of Negro teachers to receive the same pay as white teachers, the right of Negroes to buy property and live anywhere in cities, and the right of Negro children and youths to the same education as white children and youths in the public educational institutions in the southern states where separate systems of education exist. Since World War II, the Association has carried the battle against segregated public educational institutions to the United States Supreme Court and won.

In the course of these struggles, especially during the past two decades, there have been demands upon the leadership of the NAACP that it orient its policy toward the labor movement. The Association has had to take cognizance of the upsurge of the Negro masses which resulted in the "March-on-Washington" movement under A. Philip Randolph (the head of the Pullman Porters Union) that brought about the issuance of Executive Order 8802 by President Roosevelt forbidding contractors to discriminate against workers "because of race, creed, color, or national origin."[29] Although the Association was willing to fight for equal employment opportunities for the Negro, it refused to change the general orientation of its program. It continued to hold to its middle-class outlook as the defender of the rights of Negroes as American citizens. It carefully avoided any association of its program with purely working-class or "leftist" movements. In recent years the Association has attempted to prevent any Communist "infiltration" by refusing to associate itself with unions or groups in which Communists might possibly be members. The Association, which began as the result of the militancy of middle-class intellectuals, has retained its middle-class outlook and supports middle-class values.

From this analysis of the various intellectual elements in the black bourgeoisie, it is clear that they are dependent primarily upon the white propertied classes. Even the NAACP, which has stood for "racial radicalism" and has received a large part of its support from Negroes, has been influenced by the middle-class outlook of its white supporters and has sought support primarily from Negroes with a middle-class outlook. While during recent years a few Negro intellectuals have escaped from the tutelage of white philanthropy, most of these have been compelled to find a living in Negro organizations with a middle-class outlook, such as the various Negro business undertakings. The "integration" of Negro intellectuals into both public and private schools and colleges has generally confirmed the faith of these intellectuals in the soundness of the middle-class way of life. "Integration" has thus tended to increase the size and influence of the black bourgeoisie, since their *social* life continues to be centered in the Negro community. Although doctors, dentists, and lawyers depend upon the Negro masses for their living and are therefore not dependent upon white philanthropy, they have generally acquired a conservative middle-class outlook on life. In fact, no group in the black bourgeoisie exhibits its conservative outlook more than the doctors, who are generally opposed to any tendency towards socialism, especially "socialized" medicine, which would benefit the Negro masses.

## 3. Serving Two Masters

Since the wealth of the black bourgeoisie is too inconsequential for this class to wield any political power, the role of Negro politicians has been restricted to attempting to satisfy the demands of Negro voters while acting as the servants of the political machines supported by the propertied classes in the white community. When the Negro enjoyed the right of suffrage in the South during the Reconstruction period, the Negro political leaders were a part of the Republican Party machine supported by northern industrial capitalism. The state constitutions which the Negro leaders helped to draw up embodied middle-class interests and ideals. With the exception of a few political leaders who were concerned with making land available for the freedmen, the Negroes' political leaders, many of whom belonged to the class of Negroes who were free before the Civil War, were interested primarily in securing civil and political rights for the freedmen.

After the disfranchisement of the Negro in the South, the Republican Party continued to maintain a mere skeleton of an organization in most of the southern States.[30] In these organizations, which played no real role in local political struggles, Negro politicians continued to have influence. Although the Republican Party organizations did not have much influence locally except in the matter of federal appointments, they were important in the Republican National Conventions where candidates were nominated for the presidency and vice-presidency of the United States. A candidate who could be sure of the support of the southern delegates to the Republican National Convention would have a good chance of securing the nomination. The only rewards that Negroes received for their support of the Republican Party were a few federal appointments that went to middle-class Negroes. The most important rewards included the appointment of Negroes as minister to Liberia, as recorder of deeds in the District of Columbia, and as registrar of the United States Treasury. A few Negroes were also appointed as consular agents, postmasters in small towns, and as a collector of a port until President Taft inaugurated the policy of not appointing Negroes to posts in the South because of the opposition of the southern whites. These appointments did not affect the economic or social welfare of the Negro in American life, though Negro leaders made the appointments appear to be of great importance to the Negro. Southern Negro politicians continued to be the most important political leaders among Negroes until the mass migrations to northern cities where the masses gained once more the right to vote.

When the Negro masses acquired the right to vote in northern cities, they continued for a while to give their support to the Republican Party, chiefly on sentimental grounds, though there were some good reasons for their sentimental attachment to the Republican Party. The Republican Party was the party of Lincoln; it was the party which had given them their freedom. The Democratic Party was the party of the southern white men who had been responsible for lynching, disfranchisement, and segregation.[31] Negroes had respect for the words of the great Negro abolitionist leader, Frederick Douglass, who once said, "The Republican Party is the ship. All else is the open sea." But gradually the Negro masses began to demand more than the appointment of middle-class Negroes to honorific posts. A part of their re-education was due to the activities of the Communist Party.[32] The Communists began to attack the religiosity and other-wordly outlook of the Negro masses. They organized Negroes in demonstrations against racial discrimination; they nominated Negroes for political office; they gave special attention to Negro workers in their attempt to capture organized labor. However, the Communists succeeded only in enlisting the support of relatively small numbers of Negroes. The small gains which the Communists were able to make resulted in an anti-Communist campaign on the part of the municipal authorities and middle-class Negro leaders, especially the Negro preachers. Negroes who were active in Communist activities were subjected to special brutality on the part of the police.

Because of their traditional religious background, the Negro masses were easily persuaded by Negro preachers that the irreligious Communists were using Negroes as tools.

The Communists had less influence in directing the political development of the Negroes than did the inauguration of the New Deal program during the Depression years. The situation in Chicago provides an excellent study of the change in the Negro's political outlook. At the time of the presidential election in 1932, less than a fourth of the Negro vote as compared with three-fifths of the white vote in Chicago went to Roosevelt.[33] But in 1933, when more than 80,000 Negroes or 34.4 of the entire Negro population were on relief, Negroes began to shift their support to the Democratic Party which utilized its strategic position to capture Negro votes. In the 1935 election of the Democratic mayor, four-fifths of the Negro vote went to the Democratic candidate; and in 1936 half of the Negroes voted for Roosevelt. From then on the Negro voters supported the Demrocratic candidates. Oscar DePriest, a leading Negro Republican, had been elected to the United States Congress in 1928; but in 1934 Arthur Mitchell was elected to Congress on the Democratic ticket and thus became the first Negro Democratic congressman in the history of the United States.

The political leaders who have emerged as a consequence of the new role of Negroes in the political life of America are men and women with a purely middle-class outlook. In the rough and tumble politics of American cities, it has often been Negroes associated with the underworld who have been able to organize the Negro voters and wring concessions from white society.[34] These Negro leaders often operate behind the façade of a legitimate business, very frequently the undertaking business. The undertaking business brings them into intimate contact with the Negro masses. Among the Negro masses they gain a reputation for generosity and humanity by giving money to the poor and to churches and by enabling criminals to escape punishment. Behind the façade of their legitimate business, they carry on illegitimate businesses such as gambling, vice, and the lottery known as the "numbers." Therefore, their interest in the political machines is mainly to secure protection for their business enterprises. They often make financial contributions to both the Democratic and Republican Party machines in order to insure protection for their businesses. Their political affiliation or leadership has no relation to the needs of the Negro masses.

Except in the case of a crisis such as that created by the Depression when the Negro masses changed their political affiliation, the Negro politician may even mobilize the masses to vote against their economic interests.[35] In his role as leader, the Negro politician attempts to accommodate the demands of the Negro masses to his personal interests which are tied up with the political machines. He may secure the appointment of a few middle-class Negroes to positions in the municipal government. But when it comes to the fundamental interests of the Negro masses as regards employment, housing, and health, his position is determined by the political machine which represents the propertied classes of the white community. The position which the Negro political leader generally occupies in relation to the Negro masses and the dominant white community is shown in the following typical case. (See Figure I.)

The economic and political life of this small northern city, which borders a southern State, is dominated by a large manufacturing corporation.[36] This corporation provides employment for many Negroes as unskilled laborers and a large proportion of the whites as professional and white-collar workers. The white political leader is an official of the large corporation. At the same time, he is the owner of several local business enterprises including a cinema and a restaurant, neither of which admits Negroes. The white political leader finances the business enterprises of the Negro political leader who owns a cinema attended solely by Negroes. When the Negroes started a campaign for their admission to the "white" cinema and the "white" restaurant, the Negro political leader discouraged them and urged them to be loyal to Negro business enterprises. On the national scene, the white political leader played the role of a friend of Negroes. He is influential in securing a contribution from the large corporation to a fund-raising campaign for Negro education, of which he is a

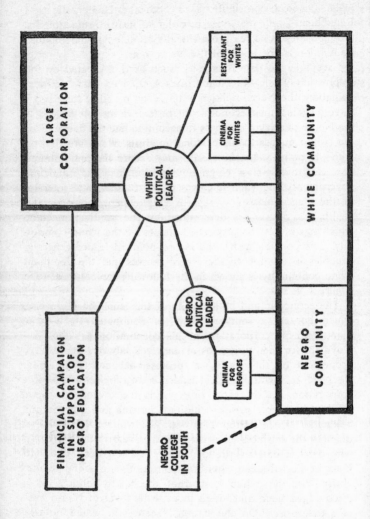

director. Moreover, he consented to become a trustee of a Negro college in the South which receives money from the fund-raising campaign. In the eyes of the black bourgeoisie of this city, some of whom send their children to the Negro college, he is a friend of the Negro. The few Negro intellectuals who have dared to express disapproval of the existing system of control over race relations have been labeled Communists.

In this chapter we have shown the role of the black bourgeoisie in the power structure of the Negro community and in the power structure of the more inclusive American community. We shall see in the following chapter how, in its rise to power in the Negro community, the black bourgeoisie has broken with the traditional background of the Negro and rejected its social heritage.

# Chapter V

## Break with the Traditional Background

THE BLACK BOURGEOISIE has been uprooted from its "racial" tradition and as a consequence has no cultural roots in either the Negro or the white world. In seeking to conform to bourgeois ideals and standards of behavior, this class in the Negro community has sloughed off the genteel tradition of the small upper class which had its roots among the Negroes who were free before the Civil War. But more important still, the black bourgeoisie has rejected the folk culture of the Negro masses. The artistic creations of the leaders of the Negro Renaissance in the nineteen twenties, who turned to the black masses for inspiration, were regarded largely with indifference by the increasing number of Negroes who were acquiring a middle-class outlook on life. As a consequence of their isolation, the majority of the black bourgeoisie live in a cultural vacuum and their lives are devoted largely to fatuities.

## 1. Passing of the Gentleman and the Peasant

There have been only two really vital cultural traditions in the social history of the Negro in the United States: one being the genteel tradition of the small group of mulattoes who assimilated the morals and manners of the slaveholding aristocracy; and the other, the culture of the black folk who gave the world the Spirituals. The genteel tradition flourished especially in such large communities of free mulattoes as those in Charleston, South Carolina, and New Orleans, Louisiana.[1] It was maintained by those mulatto families that had acquired as a part of their family traditions the patterns of behavior which were associated with the ideal of the southern lady and southern gentleman. Some families took pride in the fact that a mulatto ancestor could not be distinguished in his physical appearance, dress, manners, and speech from his white half-brother. As a rule these families formed a closed circle from which were excluded all who could not boast of similar ancestry and did not conform to the same standards of morals and manners. They were exceedingly self-conscious of their "culture" which consisted of the enjoyment of English and, in Louisiana, French classical literature and music. Sometimes they maintained literary societies in which they could enjoy and foster their "culture." Many of these families migrated before the Civil War to the North, where they formed a small upper class that boasted of its genteel traditions. Even when they could no longer make a living as independent tradesmen and artisans as they had done in the South, they continued to be "ladies" and "gentlemen" while gaining a livelihood as stewards in a club or in other fields of personal and domestic service.

After the Civil War, the free mulatto class continued to hold itself aloof from the masses of freedmen. In Louisiana, the hostility of some members of this class to the newly emancipated blacks was so great that they opposed giving political rights to the freedmen. But generally the free mulatto class and its descendants assumed as far as possible positions of leadership among the Negro masses. This did not break down the traditional barriers to easy social intercourse and marriage. Even in their religious affiliations, the descendants of the free mulattoes held aloof from the Negro masses. They generally affiliated with the Episcopal, Congregational, Presbyterian, and the Catholic Churches, while Negro masses, as we have seen, were affiliated with the Baptist and Methodist Churches. The descendants of the free mulattoes became, after the Civil War, the core of a small upper class which undertook to maintain the American pattern of family life and conventional sex mores. In some small communities in the South, a single family with this social and cultural background would live in complete isolation rather than associate with the masses of Negroes.

These families were able to maintain their ascendancy in the Negro community until their privileged position was destroyed by changes in Negro life.[2] As the Negro masses acquired education, they began gradually to flaunt the standards of behavior and values represented by the genteel tradition. The ascendancy of the "gentleman" was not completely undermined until the mass migrations of Negroes to cities and the resulting accelerated occupational differentiation of the Negro population. Sometimes these old "genteel" families sought to preserve their traditions by withdrawing from the competition with the new professional classes in the Negro community. In their quiet, obscure lives they expressed often their contempt for the black upstarts who, in their view, and often in fact, possessed neither morals nor manners. But more often the members of this class, which regarded the genteel tradition as its most precious heritage, had to come to terms with the representatives of the Negro masses who had acquired an education, especially a professional education, or had become successful in business. The attitude of those who came to terms with the successful members of the rising black masses was expressed by a young mulatto college student, who was a descendant of a prominent free mulatto family. When asked how she felt when a big, ill-mannered Negro male student addressed her rudely and tossed her about, replied, "Well, since I have got to live with these niggers, I might as well act like one."

On the whole, the tradition of the gentleman has ceased to have influence on either the manners or morals of the Negro community. In the Negro colleges, it is futile for teachers to exhort the students to behave like "ladies and gentlemen." In the highest "social circles" the tradition of the gentleman has become the source of amusement. Even when the term is used, it is quite devoid of meaning since it refers neither to morals nor manners.

Let us turn to the other cultural tradition, which represents the social heritage of the Negro masses, and see what changes it has undergone in recent decades. The folk culture of the American Negro developed out of his experiences on American soil. Whatever elements of African culture might have survived enslavement became merged with the Negro's experiences in the new environment and lost their original meaning. From the beginning the Negro had to learn the language of his masters and there was no chance to preserve

African languages except in some isolated areas, as for example, along the coasts of South Carolina and Georgia and the neighboring islands.[3] The character which the Negro family acquired under the system of slavery was due to the exigencies of servitude rather than surviving African patterns of behavior.[4] In a situation where no legal recognition of the family existed, the dominant position of the woman in the Negro family was due to the concession that had to be made to the needs of the children as well as to the attachment of mothers to their offspring. Even in the matter of religion, there are no evidences of African survivals as in the West Indies and in Brazil. Moreover, when the folk beliefs of the Negro are studied, it it difficult to disentagle the African elements from European folklore and practices and those folk beliefs which are a product of the American experience.[5]

What, then, were some of the salient features of the folk culture of the Negro before it was disrupted by economic and social changes during the past several decades? In the Cotton Belt, the main area in which the folk cultures had flourished, the Negro was not rooted to the soil in the sense in which the European peasant has been rooted to the soil. Nor have they been rooted to the soil as the Negroes in Haiti, where a landowning peasantry has preserved over five or more generations a cultural heritage embodying many African elements.[6] Because of the requirements of a commercial system of agriculture, there has been considerable physical mobility, especially since Emancipation. Nevertheless, in his social isolation in the rural South, the Negro developed a way of life which was essentially a folk culture.

The folk culture of the Negro was associated with the church, which has been the most important institution in the rural communities of the South. In fact, the community derived its name from the church, most often, Baptist or Methodist, and the location of the membership of a particular church defined the limits of the communal life. It has been in the church that the Negro has found a meaning for his existence and it was the church that enlisted his deepest loyalties. The church set up and defined the norms of moral conduct and provided the necessary discipline to enforce its rules of behavior. It was thus the chief source of social control in the Negro world, of which the whites took no notice except as their interests were affected.

Next to the church in importance and generally associated with the churches were the numerous mutual aid societies. These societies, often know as "sickness and burial" societies, which provided for the Negro in time of crisis, reveal their religious nature in their names, as for example, "Brothers and Sisters of Charity," and "Builders of the Walls of Jerusalem." In those areas where there were organizations such as the Masons, Odd Fellows, or Knights of Pythias, they were evidence of the influence of the outside world.

It was in the church that Negro Spirituals, or religious folk songs, were born. In these religious folk songs the Negro attempted to find meaning for his existence and at the same time an escape from his tragic fate. Many of these religious folk songs were sermons which were "sung-preached" by some master-singer who was joined by the congregation.[7] He clothed the hopes and yearnings of the Negro in the imagery and allegories of the Bible. In his Spirituals the Negro expressed his conception of the creation of man and the mystery of death and the hope of a better fate beyond the grave. But there was also a note of protest against the hard lot of the Negro in this world.

The Spirituals reflected, on the whole, the philosophy of life of the Negro folk. This philosophy represented an attitude of resignation in face of a hard fate—the struggle to make a living and realize himself in a world dominated by the white man. It was otherwordly in that it looked to another world for the attainment of these ends and an escape from the evils of the present world. However, not all the evils of the present world were the work of men or the result of natural forces; they were often the work of supernatural forces or evil spirits. Consequently, many of the folk practices of the Negro were magical formulae and rituals for dealing with the evil forces of the supernatural world. These folk beliefs and practices reveal the essentially religious, as opposed to the secular, character of the isolated social world of the Negro folk before the changes occurred in Negro life as the result of two World Wars.

The folk tradition of the Negro, like the genteel tradition, has been dissipated or transformed as the result of migration and urbanization. During their wanderings, the Negro folk have created the Blues, which tell of their disillusionments and nostalgic yearnings for the sympathy and understanding of the world of the folk which they have left. The secular folk songs of these black troubadours in American industrial society are living records of the reactions of the uprooted black folk in the world of the city.[8] In the countless "storefront" churches of northern cities, the Negro migrant has vainly attempted to cling to the traditional religious life of the rural South. But more often with the loss of his simple faith, in the world of the city he has sought salvation in the various religious cults, some with nationalistic aims, which are indicative of his gropings to find an escape from the white man's world.[9] His mutual aid societies, which once provided protection in time of crisis, have lost their meaning in a world where social assistance is provided by great impersonal organizations. As the result of contacts with the public school, the children of the folk have sloughed off the folk beliefs of their parents and learned the secular, scientific techniques of survival in the urban environment. Thus, instead of their old resignation toward the world, the Negro masses are acquiring a confidence in the efficacy of their efforts through the use of the ballot and in joining with fellow-workers in the labor unions.

## 2. The Renaissance That Failed

As the result of the uprooting of the traditions of the gentleman and the peasant, two movements of unique significance developed among Negroes. One was the only truly nationalistic movement ever to appear among Negroes, and the other a literary and artistic renaissance which turned to the black masses for inspiration.

The movement with nationalistic aims was known as the "Garvey Movement," taking its name from its leader, Marcus Garvey, a West Indian Negro. It was no accident that this movement was led by a West Indian Negro. Garvey, who was apparently of pure Negro ancestry, was born in Jamaica in 1885, where he had undertaken to organize a Negro Improvement Association, a scheme which he had conceived during his travels in England and France.[10] After his failure in Jamaica, he came to the United States during the first World War. His attempt to create a similar movement in the United States did not meet with much success until large numbers of Negroes began to migrate to New York City from the West Indies. With a large nucleus of West Indian Negroes in Harlem, he began to make an appeal on purely racial grounds to the Negro masses, especially the disillusioned Negroes from the South who had failed to find the Promised Land which they sought in the North.

The program of the "Garvey Movement" was based upon the thesis that since the Negro would never achieve equality and justice in a white man's country, the only solution of his problem was the establishment of an independent nation in Africa.[11] In his appeal to the masses of American as well as West Indian Negroes, Garvey exhibited a keen understanding of the hurt self-esteem and frustrations of black men in the United States.[12] He launched a newspaper, *The Negro World*, in which he not only made articulate the resentments of the Negro but provided a vision of a new Promised Land in Africa. Through his speeches in Liberty Hall in Harlem, in the literature which he disseminated, and in the organization he set up he created a new valuation of everything black or Negro. He created a military organization which was to be the vanguard of the African army and he organized a corps of "Black Cross Nurses." He invented honors and distinctions which caused the Negro to feel that he was a part of a great cause. He set up stores and restaurants and started a project for a fleet of steamships that would bind the Negroes in America to Africa. Although the movement had its largest following in New York City, it spread to Chicago, Detroit, and Philadelphia, and even attracted some Negroes in southern cities. But the movement collapsed when Garvey was sent to the federal penitentiary in Atlanta, Georgia, for using the mails for fraudulent purposes in promoting his projected steamship lines to Africa. The messianic element in his movement is revealed in the message to his followers that appeared in *The Negro World* under the caption, "If I Die in Atlanta," in which he wrote: "Look for me in the whirlwind or the storm, look for me all around you, for with God's grace, I shall come and bring with me the countless millions of black slaves who have died in America and the West Indies and the millions in Africa to aid you in the fight for liberty, freedom and life."[13]

The Garvey Movement did not attract any support from the emerging black bourgeoisie. In fact, Garvey, who had been acquainted with the deep cleavage between the mulatto middle class and the black masses in Jamaica, made the mistake of attacking Negro leaders with white ancestry in the United States, where even the remotest Negro ancestry classified a person as a Negro. But if he had not made this mistake, he would still not have enlisted the support of the increasing numbers of Negroes who were acquiring middle-class status. They did not only regard his programs as fantastic, but they did not want to associate with his illiterate and poor black followers, especially since West Indians were prominent in the movement.[14]

The young intellectuals among the emerging black bourgeoisie, who called themselves "the New Negro," began expressing their orientation to American life in what has come to be known as the Negro Renaissance. The "first fruits" of the Negro Renaissance were published in *The New Negro*, edited by Alain Locke, in 1925. It is significant that one of the contributors to this volume was James Weldon Johnson, whose poem, "Lift Every Voice and Sing," written originally for school children in Jacksonville, Florida, was becoming a sort of national Negro hymn. In his poem Johnson had endowed the enslavement of the Negro and his struggle for freedom with a certain nobility. His book, *Fifty Years and Other Poems*, was published in 1917 when the migration of southern Negroes to northern cities was at its height. One poem in this book expressed the dominant spirit of the Negro Renaissance. It was entitled "O Black and Unknown Bards," in which the poet asks:

How came your lips to touch the sacred fire?
How, in your darkness, did you come to know
The power and beauty of the minstrel's lyre?

In this poem Johnson was expressing a re-evaluation of the Spirituals which many Negroes had rejected as a part of the heritage of slavery. According to Locke, the editor of *The New Negro,* the younger generation had achieved an objective attitude toward life, and in "shaking off the psychology of imitation and implied inferiority," the Negro was achieving "something like a spiritual emancipation."[15] In more concrete terms, Sterling Brown has decribed the Negro Renaissance as being concerned with "(1) a discovery of Africa as a source of race pride, (2) a use of Negro heroes and heroic episodes from American history, (3) propaganda of protest, (4) a treatment of the Negro masses (frequently of the folk, less often of the workers) with more understanding and less apology, (5) franker and deeper self-revelation. Some of this subject matter called for a romantic approach, some for a realistic."[16]

As one studies the literary and artistic productions of the Negro Renaissance, there is an indication that Negro intellectuals and artists were acquiring a more objective attitude toward their experience in American life and that they were overcoming their feelings of inferiority. Much of the fiction of the Negro Renaissance indicates not only an objective attitude toward the past but a sympathetic understanding of the lives of the Negro masses. Likewise, in the poetry of Countee Cullen, Langston Hughes and others, there is no apology for the free, unconventional life of the Negro masses. The distinctive contributions of Sterling Brown, who was identified with the Negro Renaissance, were his poems which revealed the ironic humor of the Negro folk who had left their rural background to wander and work in the white man's civilization.[17]

The "spiritual emancipation" of which Locke wrote did not affect the emerging black bourgeoisie. They did not react, however, as the small Negro elite, comprised mostly of mulattoes, had reacted at the beginning of the century against the dialect poetry of Paul Laurence Dunbar, the first Negro poet to treat with humor and sympathetic understanding the Negro rural folk.[18] They were critical of what they called "common Negroes" in literature and, on the whole, the black bourgeoisie either ignored the Negro Renaissance or, when they exhibited any interest in it, they revealed their ambivalence towards the Negro masses. Although very few of the increasing number of middle-class Negroes read the literary productions of the Negro Renaissance or saw the work of the artists identified with it, they would refer to the achievements of this period as a defense against the implications of their racial inferiority.

## 3. Mobility and Money

When Harlem in New York City became the Mecca of the "New Negro" and the center of the Negro Renaissance, the capital of the black bourgeoisie was Durham, North Carolina.[19] In this city were located the most spectacular achievements of Negroes in the field of business enterprise: the North Carolina Mutual Life Insurance Company, the Mechanics and Farmers Bank, the Bankers Fire Insurance Company, and the National Negro Finance Corporation. These enterprises had grown out of the pioneering efforts of men who had had little experience with business but had been inspired by the current faith, promulgated by Negro leaders, that business enterprise would open the way to equality and acceptance in white America. One of the pioneers had started out as a barber and with his savings had bought a fraternal organization. Later he joined with a physician and a manager of a grocery store in promoting the North Carolina Mutual Life Insurance Company. Success in this undertaking led them into other forms of business whenever an opportunity to promote some enterprise appeared.

Although the promoters of these enterprises were inspired by the spirit of modern business, they exhibited at the beginning of their careers the old-fashioned virtues of the old middle class. Their lives reveal none of the Negro's love of leisure and enjoyment of life. They were frugal and abstemious in their habits. They strove to attain middle-class respectability through industry and morality. They maintained middle-class ideals. In fact, in the nineteen twenties the children of the founders of these Negro enterprises were beginning to assume positions of control in these business undertakings. Because of the influence of these families, the Negro community in Durham with its fine homes, exquisite churches, and middle-class respectability was regarded as the capital of the black bourgeoisie.

As the black bourgeoisie has grown in size and influence, Durham has ceased to enjoy the distinction of being its "capital." The Negro communities in Chicago and Detroit have both claimed to have become the center of the black bourgeoisie. In either case the shift of the "capital" of the black bourgeoisie from a small southern city to a northern metropolis is indicative of the change in the character and outlook of this class. Although the younger generations of Negro businessmen in Durham had acquired more thoroughly than the pioneers the psychology of the modern businessman, they were still influenced by the older traditions that had grown up in the Negro community. They still conformed to the tradition of the gentleman which lingered and shaped their morals and manners. They still felt some identification with the Negro masses despite the fact that their interests might be opposed to those of the masses. This was due partly to the fact that they as well as the Negro masses lived under a system of rigid racial segregation. Moreover, they were more closely identified with the institutions in the Negro communities which were supported by the masses. On the other hand, the black bourgeoisie which has become important in recent years, has tended to break completely with the traditions of the Negro. As the system of rigid racial segregation has broken down, the black bourgeoisie has lost much of its feeling of racial solidarity with the Negro masses. In the metropolitan areas of the North where there are increasing opportunities for employment and earning money, social mobility, which means primarily the attainment of middle-class status, has become a question of the amount of money which one has to spend. When a French sociologist, on a study tour in the United States, saw the emergence of the black bourgeoisie in northern cities, he observed that they were "really colored Babbitts."[20]

The break with traditional values is seen in the changes in the canons of respectability. Among the older upper-class families in the Negro community, who really stood for a middle-class way of life, the canons of respectability required a stable family life and conventional sex behavior. On the other hand, among the new black bourgeoisie these values are regarded as "old fashioned" virtues and there is much confusion in thinking and behavior with reference to these values. Divorces and scandals in family and sex behavior do not affect one's social status; rather the notoriety which one acquires in such cases adds to one's prestige. The change in attitudes towards the "old fashioned" bourgeois values is due largely to the fact that the new bourgeoisie is recruited from those elements in the Negro population among whom these virtues never existed and that money has become the chief requirement for social acceptance.[21]

Among the professional classes in the Negro community, actors and entertainers are relatively numerous and have the largest incomes. The actors and entertainers, who very often have a lower-class background in the social hierarchy of the Negro community, exercise a far greater influence upon the morals and manners in the Negro community than actors and entertainers in the white community. Their prestige is owing partly to the glamor of their personalities, but more especially to their financial success, which is due to their support by the white world. The black bourgeoisie is also being recruited from the successful underworld Negroes, who have gained their money from gambling, prostitution, bootlegging, and the "numbers." The old upper class in the Negro community erected an impenetrable barrier between themselves and Negroes who represented the "sporting" and criminal world. Since such Negroes were generally able to handle more money than the majority of Negroes, they always constituted a threat to the respectable way of life cherished by the old middle classes. As the result of urbanization, which upset the old class structure of the Negro community, the "sporting" and criminal elements began to acquire a dominant position among Negroes.[22]

With the emergence of the new black bourgeoisie, the standards of consumption which the "sporting" and criminal elements are able to maintain have become the measure of success among the black middle class. The standards which they set are emulated by Negroes in the professional classes—doctors, dentists and lawyers, and even teachers as far as they are able to do so. But more important still, in order to secure the money necessary to maintain these standards, Negro professional men engage in the same "rackets" as the successful Negroes in the underworld. Consequently, among the black bourgeoisie an expensive automobile, a "palatial" residence, and a yacht bring more recognition to a doctor than some achievement in medicine. At the summer resorts where the black bourgeoisie gather to display their wealth, the descendants of the old respectable families must defer to the underworld elements, who, through their money, have risen to the top of Negro "society."

The deeper significance of the break with the Negro's traditional background is revealed in the religious outlook and behavior of the black bourgeoisie. As we have seen in the last chapter, in moving up the social ladder Negroes have tended to leave the Baptist and Methodist churches and have affiliated with the Episcopal, Congregational, and Presbyterian churches, and to a less extent with the Catholic Church. In the past this usually meant that Negroes who were rising in the social scale mainly because of education were seeking a form of religious expression more in accord with their developed religious sentiments. But with the emergence of the new black bourgeoisie, a radical change has occurred in the religious outlook and practices of those who have risen to the top of the social pyramid. Religion has become secular and practical in the sense that it is no longer concerned with the mystery and meaning of life and that it has become divorced from any real religious sentiment. The church of the Negro masses, like the fraternal organizations, is regarded as an instrument for the advancement of the interests of the black bourgeoisie, while the churches with which the black bourgeoisie affiliate are regarded as part of the social paraphernalia of this class. They give money to the churches of the masses as an expenditure for good "public relations." The contributions which they make to the churches with which they themselves are affiliated have become a form of conspicuous consumption. But they have little time or sympathy for the traditional religion of the Negro as expressed in the Spirituals. Such religion, according to their view, belongs to the past which should be forgotten.

Having abandoned their social heritage and being rejected by the white world, the black bourgeoisie have an intense feeling of inferiority, constantly seek various forms of recognition and place great value upon status symbols in order to compensate for their inferiority complex. In the following chapter, we shall trace the sources of this inferiority complex and study the struggle of the black bourgeoisie to achieve status and recognition in American society.

## Chapter VI

## Inferiority Complex and Quest for Status

THE ENTIRE HISTORY of the Negro in the United States has been of a nature to create in the Negro a feeling of racial inferiority. During the more than two centuries of enslavement by the white man, every means was employed to stamp a feeling of natural inferiority in the Negro's soul. Christianity and the Bible were utilized both to prove and to give divine sanction to his alleged racial inferiority or, as some contended, his exclusion from the races of mankind. When the system of slavery was uprooted in a Second American Revolution, it appeared for a brief period that the Negro might receive recognition as a man. But as the result of the unresolved class conflict in which the democratic forces in the South were defeated, the demagogues who became the leaders of the disinherited whites but really served the interests of the propertied classes made the Negro the scapegoat. A legalized system of racial segregation was established which stigmatized the Negro as unfit for human association, and every type of propaganda was employed to prove that the Negro was morally degenerate and intellectually incapable of being educated. Living constantly under the domination and contempt of the white man, the Negro came to believe in his own inferiority, whether he ignored or accepted the values of the white man's world. The black bourgeoisie—the element which has striven more than any other element among Negroes to make itself over in the image of the white man—exhibits most strikingly the inferiority complex of those who would escape their racial identification.

## 1. A Chattel in an Alien Land

When the Constitution of the United States was adopted, it provided that the number of representatives from each state in the House of Representatives should be determined by adding to the whole "Number of free Persons, including those bound to service for a Term of Years, and excluding Indians not taxed, three-fifths of all other Persons."[1] "Three-fifths of all other Persons" referred, of course, to the Negroes, and the agreement to count the Negro as three-fifths of a person was a compromise between the position that slaves should not be counted at all and the desire on the part of the southern states to have as large representation as possible. Although the Negro was finally counted as three-fifths of a person for the purposes of representation in Congress, his actual status as a person in the southern society was probably more accurately described by the Charleston *Mercury,* which stated that the Negro was as much "an article of commerce" as "the sugar and molasses" which he produced.[2] Despite the "human" relations which developed between Negroes and whites on the plantations where a paternalistic type of control developed, the Negro was, nevertheless, an "article of commerce" or an animate tool, according to Aristotle's definition of a slave. If any recognition were shown him as a person, it was conceded to a person who represented a lower and inferior order of mankind.

During and for a brief period following the American Revolution, some of the leaders who had acquired French ideas concerning human rights expressed their opposition to the enslavement of the Negro. For example, Thomas Jefferson attacked slavery in his original draft of the Declaration of Independence, in which he declared that the king of England had "waged cruel war against human nature itself" in supporting the slave trade.[3] Such sentiments in regard to the enslavement of the Negro were not shared by the plantation owners in the lower South. Jefferson was a Virginian, and the plantation system of agriculture was becoming unprofitable in Virginia. When, as the result of technological developments in the textile industries of England, there was a great demand for cotton, and Eli Whitney perfected his cotton gin, the "idealism" concerning human rights ceased to have any reference to the Negro except among a small group of whites in New England. During the period from 1790 to 1808, the year in which importation of slaves became illegal, over 100,000 slaves were brought to the United States, and, because of the failure of the federal government to suppress the slave trade after 1808, between 250,000 and 300,000 were smuggled into the country.[4]

Reduced to a chattel in an alien land, the enslaved Negro was not only "detribalized" as the African who has had contact with European civilization, but he was annihilated as a person. Although the detribalized African may take up permanent residence in a town and sever relations with his chief and his relatives, there is always the tribal organization to which he can return or the traditional culture with which he can identify.[5] The enslavement of the Negro in the United States destroyed not only his family ties and his household gods; it effaced whatever memories of the African homeland that had survived the Middle Passage. The destruction of a common tradition and religious beliefs and practices reduced the Negro to a mere "atom" without a personality or social identity. The main significance of the proselytizing of the Baptist and Methodist missionaries was that Christianity was presented to the slaves in a simple, emotional appeal that provided a release for their frustrated and repressed lives. More than that, it established a bond of union among the slaves and provided them with a meaning of their existence in an alien world.

Although Christianity offered the Negro an interpretation of his existence in an alien world, it did not undertake to change his earthly condition as regards his enslavement. When for economic reasons, during the seventeenth century the Negro indentured servant lost the status which white indentured servants had and became a servant for life, or a slave, the colonial legislatures made it clear that that conversion to Christianity meant freedom not for the body in this world, but for the soul in the after life. Nor did the Society for the Propagation of the Gospel in Foreign Parts, which began its missionary efforts among Negroes in the eighteenth century, offer the Negro slave any escape from subordination to the white man in this world.[6] Among the various Christian missionaries who undertook the conversion of the Negroes during most of the eighteenth century, only the Quakers, who generally met with opposition among the planters, were in favor of the emancipation of the slaves.[7] However, none of the proselyting faiths attracted large numbers of Negroes until the Baptists and Methodists began their missionary efforts during the closing years of the eighteenth century. In the beginning, the Baptist and Methodist missionaries, who brought their message of salvation to the poor and outcast, were in favor of the emancipation of the slaves, but soon they accommodated their message of salvation to the earthly condition of the Negro slave.

Not only did Christianity fail to offer the Negro hope of freedom in this world, but the manner in which Christianity was communicated to him tended to degrade him. The Negro was taught that his enslavement was due to the fact that he had been cursed by God. His very color was a sign of the curse which he had received as a descendant of Ham. Parts of the Bible were carefully selected to prove that God had intended that the Negro should be the servant of the white man and that he would always be a "hewer of wood and drawer of water." While such was being taught the slave, some of the leading ministers of the South were setting forth the same doctrine in books for the American public. One of these books, written by a Presbyterian minister and entitled *The Christian Doctrine of Slavery*, stated that "It may be, that *Christian slavery* is God's solution of the problem [relation of labor and capital] about which the wisest statesmen of Europe confess themselves at fault."[8] Another leading minister published a book entitled *Slavery Ordained of God* in which he defended the doctrine that "slavery is ordained of God, and to continue for the good of the slave, the good of the master, the good of the whole American family, until another and better destiny may be unfolded."[9] These theological justifications of the enslavement of the Negro gave religious support to the philosophical justifications of slavery, the most celebrated of which was that by a Professor of History, Metaphysics and Political Law at William and Mary College, Virginia. In a book published in 1832, he justified the enslavement of the Negro on the grounds that the Negro possessed the strength and form of a man, but had the intellect of a child and was therefore unfit for freedom.[10]

Since the Negro's black skin was a sign of the curse of God and of his inferiority to the white man, therefore a light complexion resulting from racial mixture raised a mulatto above the level of the unmixed Negro. Although mulattoes were not always treated better than the blacks, as a rule they were taken into the household or were apprenticed to a skilled artisan. Partly because of the differential treatment accorded the mulattoes, but more especially because of general degradation of the Negro as a human being, the Negro of mixed ancestry thought of himself as being superior to the unmixed Negro. His light complexion became his most precious possession. Witness, for example, the typical case of the mulatto slave begging Frances Kemble that she "be put to some other than field labor because hoeing in the field was so hard on her *on account of her color*."[11] Concerning the prestige which white "blood" conferred, Miss Kemble observed that the slaves accepted the contempt of their masters to such an extent that "they profess, and really seem to feel it for themselves, and the faintest admixture of white blood in their veins appears at once, by common consent of their own race, to raise them in the scale of humanity."[12]

The nearly 600,000 mulattoes among the somewhat less than 4.5 million Negroes in the United States in 1860 were the result of the sexual association of white men and Negro women.[13] The character of the sexual association between white men and Negro women ranged from rape based upon physical force or the authority of the master to voluntary surrender on the part of the Negro women.[14] Voluntary surrender on the part of the Negro woman was due at times to mutual attraction, but the prestige of the white race was often sufficient to secure compliance on their part. In giving themselves to their white masters there were certain concrete advantages to be gained, such as freedom from the drudgery of field work, better food and clothing, and the prospect that their half-white children would enjoy certain privileges and perhaps be emancipated. As the mulatto class grew in the South, many slaveholders, if married, set up a separate household for their black, but more often, mulatto concubines. In some cases they lived a monogamous life with their mulatto mistress or concubine, legal marriage being forbidden. But even under the most favorable conditions, the woman and her offspring were stigmatized because of their Negro ancestry.

It was out of such association that the communities of free mulattoes grew up in the South. In some parts of the South they constituted a sort of lower caste, since no matter how well off they might be economically, they always bore the stigma of Negro ancestry. Even in Louisiana, where the quadroons or *gens de couleur* became wealthy and sent their children to France to be educated, they were still without political rights and could not associate with whites on a basis of equality. But they, like free mulattoes in Charleston, South Carolina, and other localities, would not associate with the blacks. The free Negroes of Charleston, who organized the Brown Fellowship Society in 1790, admitted only *brown* men.[15] This society provided for the education of the free people of color, assisted widows and orphans, and maintained a clubhouse and a cemetery for its members. They identified themselves as far as possible with the interests of the white slaveholding aristocracy and did not even permit a discussion of slavery among their members. Although they were not white, they could thank God that they were not black.

Religion and political philosophy rallied to the support of the planters in the South by confirming the racial inferiority of the Negro. This support became especially urgent as the conflict between the economic interests of the North and South became more acute, and the issue over slavery acquired a moral character. Whether the Negro was only chattel property, and, therefore, had no rights as a human being became an issue in the celebrated Dred Scott

Case which was taken to the Supreme Court. In 1857 Chief Justice Taney of the Supreme Court, which was dominated by the South, handed down the famous decision, "A Negro has no rights which a white man need respect."[16] The Court declared that in the meaning of the words "people of the United States," in the Constitution, Negroes were not included in the people of the United States. This represented the final triumph of the southern aristocracy in its struggle to dominate the United States.

## 2. Half-a-Man in a White Man's Country

The primary aim of the North in the Civil War was to save the Union. Lincoln made this clear in a letter to Horace Greeley in August, 1862, in which he stated: "My paramount object in this struggle is to save the Union, and not either to save or destroy slavery."[17] Whatever he did about slavery and Negroes was a part of his official duty and was not intended to modify his "personal wish that all men everywhere could be free."[18] Less than a month after writing this letter, he stated in a speech in Chicago that slavery was "at the root of the rebellion" and that the emancipation of the Negro would help the Union cause in Europe.[19] This growing recognition on the part of Lincoln that the emancipation of the Negro was tied up with the struggle of the North against the South was due partly to the question which had been raised concerning the employment of Negro soldiers in northern armies. In fact, the employment of Negroes as soldiers in the Union Army posed the crucial question of the future status of the Negro in American society.

Lincoln did not have much faith in the ability of Negroes to be trained as soldiers. He had stated that if Negroes were given arms, within a few weeks their arms would be in the hands of the southern rebels. Lincoln shared the prejudices of the masses of northern whites, to whom, as DuBois has well said, "the Negro was a curiosity, a sub-human minstrel, willing and naturally a slave, and treated as well as he deserved to be. He had not sense enough to revolt and help the Northern armies, even if Northern armies were trying to emancipate him, which they were not. The North shrank at the very thought of encouraging servile insurrection against the whites."[20] General Hunter, an abolitionist, had recruited Negro soldiers in South Carolina after applying in vain to Washington for reenforcements. His action provoked a long debate in Congress which resulted in the disbanding of his Negro regiment. It was only after the Emancipation Proclamation and a pressing need for manpower that the War Department authorized the employment of Negro soldiers.[21]

The general attitude of the North towards the arming of the Negro was indicated by the fact that when it was planned for the first two regiments authorized by the War Department (the Fifty-fourth and the Fifty-fifth Massachusetts regiments) to pass through New York City, the Chief of Police warned that they would be insulted, and it was necessary for these regiments to go by sea to the theatre of war in South Carolina.[22] Because of the general opposition to the enlistment of Negroes as soldiers, many difficulties beset their recruitment. It was regarded as a stigma for white officers to serve in Negro regiments. Then there was opposition in Congress to giving Negro soldiers the same pay as white soldiers. It was not until 1864 that it was finally agreed that Negro soldiers should receive the same pay as white soldiers. This is not strange in view of the fact that the Negro in the North outside of New England did not live under the same laws as the whites.[23]

Nearly 200,000 Negro soldiers served in the Civil War which became, despite the intention of the majority of northern leaders, a war of emancipation. Since the Negro had contributed to the success of northern arms, they felt that they had earned the right to freedom and citizenship. There has been an attempt to disparage the contribution of the Negro soldiers to the victory of the North, but the unprejudiced white officers who led Negro soldiers testified to their courage and efficiency.[24] This was, however, only the beginning of a campaign of disparagement of the Negro soldier which was to continue until World War II. Soon after his emancipation the Negro began to experience disillusionment about the meaning of freedom. The southern States enacted the Black Codes which really re-enslaved the Negro.[25] Restrictions were placed upon the occupations in which the freedmen could enter, provisions were made for them to be "apprenticed" to their former masters, and severe penalties provided for their failure to keep their "Labor contracts" with the planters and for being impudent to whites. It was the enactment of these Black Codes by the southern States that provided the moral justification for placing the South under military rule and using military power to guarantee the rights of the Negro as a citizen.

For a brief period, less than a decade in most southern States, the Negro enjoyed the rights of a citizen. If the Second American Revolution had not been aborted it would have established a democracy in the South in which the poor whites and black freedmen would have shared power. Leaders like Senator Charles Sumner of Massachusetts and Congressman Thaddeus Stevens of Pennsylvania wanted to divide up the plantations and create a class of black and white small farmers who would have formed the basis of this democracy. But the industrialists in the North were not interested in democracy; they were interested in the exploitation of the resources of the South and in forming an alliance with the emerging middle classes. As a consequence, northern troops were withdrawn from the South when the Negro's vote was no longer needed.[26] The so-called restoration of "white supremacy" really meant the political domination of the "Bourbons" or the alliance of the planters and the new industrial and commercial classes in the South. During the Reconstruction Period, there had never been any Negro domination in the South. Although the Republican Party in the South depended upon Negro voters, it also had southern white supporters who were called "scalawags." The race issue was utilized to defeat not only the Republican Party but the democratic upsurge which was threatened by the alliance of the black freedmen and the poor whites. Under the political dominance of the "Bourbons" the poor whites were in about the same economic condition as the freedmen.

The restoration of "white supremacy" in the South did not resolve the class conflict within the white community. This opened the way for the rise of the southern demagogues who offered a solution to the class conflict that did not threaten the economic interests of the propertied class while offering some relief to the poor whites. As we have seen in the Introduction, their program provided for the complete disfranchisement of Negroes, the diversion of public school funds from Negro schools to white schools, and the establishment of a system of legalized racial segregation. What has erroneously been called "the rise of the poor whites" in the 1890's inaugurated a period in the history of the Negro in the United States during which a studied campaign was carried on to prove that the Negro was subhuman, morally degenerate and incapable of being educated. Although the "Bourbons" had achieved political power on the racial issue, they often had as little regard for poor whites as for poor Negroes. Once in power, they were willing to leave the voteless and landless Negroes in peace. But the demagogic leaders of the poor whites carried on a ceaseless campaign of terror and vituperation against all persons of Negro descent for over a quarter of a century.

The southern white politicians who carried on this campaign had the support of the propertied classes, the newspapers, and the clergy. They carried their campaign to the halls of the Congress of the United States where they met with scarcely any opposition. The North had become weary and ashamed of its idealism about the Negro and had agreed that the South could best handle the Negro problem. At the same time the Supreme Court of the United States had been nullifying or curtailing the rights of Negroes which had been written into the Amendments of the Constitution or into laws.[27] During the 1890's two to three Negroes were lynched each week.[28] In 1898 there was a riot in Wilmington, North Carolina, during which Negroes were murdered, their property was destroyed, they were evicted from the petty offices to which they were elected, and driven from the city.[29] In regard to the Negro's fitness to vote, Senator Vardaman of Mississippi declared: "It matters not what his (the Negro's) advertised mental and moral qualifications may be. I am just as much opposed to Booker Washington as a voter, with all his Anglo-Saxon reenforcements, as I am to the cocoanut-headed, chocolate-colored, typical little coon, Andy Dotson, who blacks my shoes every morning. Neither is fit to exercise the supreme function of citizenship."[30] Then there was Senator Tillman of South Carolina who advocated the killing of 30,000 Negroes in his State and declared in a public lecture in Detroit, Michigan, that on one occasion he did not know how many Negroes he had killed.[31] In the Congress of the United States in 1898, David A. DeArmond of Missouri described Negroes as being "almost too ignorant to eat, scarcely wise enough to breathe, mere existing human machines."[32]

While public opinion and the personal attitudes of whites concerning the Negroes were being formed by politicians and newspapers, there appeared in 1900 a book entitled *The Negro a Beast,* published by the American Book and Bible House.[33] The publishers of this book stated in the preface that if this book were "considered in an intelligent and prayerful manner, that it will be to the minds of the American people like unto the voice of God from the clouds appealing to Paul on his way to Damascus." In order that the American people might be convinced of the scientific nature of the "Biblical truths" presented in this book, the author included pictures of God and an idealized picture of a white man in order to prove that white people were made in the image of God, as stated in the Bible, and a caricature of the Negro showing that he could not have been made in the image of God. This book had a wide circulation, especially among the church-going whites, and helped to fix in their minds, as it was argued in the last chapter of this book, that the Negro was not the son of Ham or even the descendant of Adam and Eve, but "simply a beast without a soul."[34]

While this book was giving a religious sanction to current beliefs concerning the inferiority of the Negro, the Negro's inferiority was being engraved in every public edifice—railroad stations, court houses, theatres—with signs showing rear entrances for Negroes or kitchens in which Negroes might be served. Moreover, in every representation of the Negro, he was pictured as a gorilla dressed up like a man. His picture was never carried in the newspapers of the South (the same rule holds today in most parts of the South) unless he had committed a crime. In the newspapers the Negro was described as burly or ape-like and even Negroes who looked like whites were represented in cartoons as black with gorilla features. All of this fitted into the stereotype which represented the Negro as subhuman or a beast, without any human qualities. This vilification of the Negro continued until the second decade of the twentieth century. A so-called authoritative study of the Negro, published as a doctoral dissertation in the Columbia University Studies in History, Economics and Public Law, accepted as scientific evidence the statement that the Negro was "as destitute of morals as any of the lower animals."[35] In the very year in which the first World War started, an advertised authority on the Negro stated in a book that the Negro was an instinctive criminal.[36] Then in 1915, an army surgeon assured the American people that "many animals below man manifest a far greater amount of real affection in their love-making than do negroes" and that it is very rare that "we see two negroes kiss each other."[37] It is not surprising that when this book was written a Negro could not sing a sentimental song on the American stage.

During this campaign to prove that the Negro was subhuman and unfit for human association, the masses of Negroes found a refuge within the isolated world of the Negro folk. Their lives revolved principally about their churches, where they sang their songs of resignation and looked forward to another world in which they might escape the contempt and disdain of the white man. The Negro who migrated to a northern city discovered that he was only half-a-man in the white man's world.[38] The educated middle-class Negroes, who had striven to conform to American ideals and had contacts with a larger social world, could not find a refuge in the world of the Negro folk. In the

South they were subject to the same Jim Crow Laws and contempt as the Negro masses, and in the North they were outsiders.[39] The mass migrations of Negroes to northern cities and the impact of two world wars upon the United States changed the relation of the Negro to American society. But Negroes have remained outsiders, who still face the problem of being integrated into American society. The black bourgeoisie, who have striven to mold themselves in the image of the white man, have not been able to escape from the mark of racial inferiority.

## 3. The Struggle for Status and Recognition

Although the old black bourgeoisie, or Negro upper class, was not able to find a refuge in the world of the Negro folk, nevertheless, they were sheltered to some extent against the contempt and terror of the white man because they lived within the segregated Negro world. Their privileged position at the top of the social pyramid behind the walls of segregation provided some compensation for their hurt self-esteem. But while the Negro folk were exposed to a greater extent to the violence of the whites, the black bourgeoisie was more exposed in a spiritual sense. Except for the economic relations with whites, the Negro folk could retreat within their own world with its peculiar religious life, recreation, and family and sex life. Moreover, since the thinking of the Negro folk was not affected as that of the black bourgeoisie by the books and papers in which the Negro's inferiority was proclaimed, the black bourgeoisie suffered spiritually not only because they were affected by ideas concerning the Negro's inferiority, but perhaps even more because they had adopted the white man's values and patterns of behavior. Consequently, they developed an intense inferiority complex and because of this inferiority complex sought compensations.

A large section of the old middle class sought compensations in their white heritage.[40] They were not merely proud of their white complexion, but they boasted of their kinship with the aristocratic whites of the South. In fact, in some cases their white ancestors had helped them to secure an education or had provided for them economically. They also sought compensations in the standards of puritanical family and sex mores, which set them apart from the black masses. But the chief compensation for their inferior status in American society was found in education. While their racial heritage and conventional standards of morality only gave them a privileged position in the Negro community, education gave them access to a world of ideas that provided an intellectual escape from their physical and social segregation in American life. Therefore, they placed an exaggerated importance upon academic degrees, especially if they were secured from white colleges in the North. If one secured the degree of doctor of philosophy in a northern university, he was regarded as a sort of genius. Consequently, for the relatively small group of educated Negroes, education was an indication of their "superior culture" and a mark of "refinement."

Education was not simply a form of compensation because it set them apart from the Negro masses; it provided a form of compensation as regards their relations with whites. They constantly asserted their educational and "cultural" superiority to the majority of the whites whose education was inferior to theirs. Whenever they had contacts with white men who called them by their first names or insulted them, they would take consolation in the fact that the white man was ignorant and could not appreciate art and literature or the things of the spirit as they could. Was not DuBois expressing this type of compensation when, while a professor of sociology in Atlanta University during the early years of the century, he wrote, "I sit with Shakespeare and he winces not. Across the color line I move arm in arm with Balzac and Dumas, where smiling men and welcoming women glide in gilded hall"?[41]

Despite their solid achievements and the satisfactions which they derived from their way of life, there was always an atmosphere of unreality surrounding the isolated life of the small black middle class. As we have seen, urbanization and the increasing occupational differentiation of the Negro population undermined the privileged position of the old middle class. But more important still, the compensations which ancestry, puritanical morals, and especially education, provided in a hostile white world were inadequate in the life of the new black bourgeoisie. Having become less isolated and thus more exposed to the contempt and hostility of the white world, but at the same time cherishing the values of the white world, the new black bourgeoisie with more money at their disposal, have sought compensations in the things that money can buy. Moreover, their larger incomes have enabled them to propagate false notions about their place in American life and to create a world of make-believe. It is to a description and analysis of this make-believe world, in which the black bourgeoisie live, that the second part of this study is devoted.

# PART TWO
# THE WORLD OF MAKE-BELIEVE

Chapter VII

# Negro Business: A Social Myth

IN THE FIRST SECTION, we saw that the capital investment represented by Negro business was insignificant from the standpoint of the American economy and that it provided an exceedingly small amount of employment and income for Negro workers. Here our purpose is to show how false ideas concerning the importance of Negro business have become a social myth and how this myth has been propagated among Negroes. This social myth has been one of the main elements in the world of "make-believe" which the black bourgeoisie has created to compensate for its feeling of inferiority in a white world dominated by business enterprise.

## 1. Origin of the Myth

When did this myth first take form? It was formulated, it should be noted, during the last decade of the nineteenth century when a legal system of racial separation and subordination was inaugurated and the hope of Negroes to attain equality in American life was crushed. The myth was created by a small group of Negro intellectuals and Negro leaders who accepted racial separation as the inevitable solution of the race problem. From the 1880's on, as Professor Harris has pointed out in his *The Negro as Capitalist*:

. . . the Negro masses, urged by their leaders, were led to place increasing faith in business and property as a means of escaping poverty and achieving economic independence. Although ostensibly sponsored as the means of self-help or racial cooperation, as it was sometimes called, through which the masses were to be economically emancipated, Negro business enterprise was motivated primarily by the desire for private profit and looked toward the establishment of a Negro capitalist employer class. One of the clearest expressions of the growing tendency to look upon the development of Negro capitalists and business enterprise as the basis of racial economic advancement is to be found in the proceedings of the Fourth Atlanta University Conference (1898) on "The Negro in Business."[1]

At this conference, the best formulation of the myth of the economic salvation of the Negro through Negro business was presented by the late John Hope, who later on, after becoming president of the Atlanta University system (exclusively for Negroes), hoped to train the future leaders of "Negro business." He stated:

Industrial education and labor unions for Negroes will not change this condition. [Displacement of Negro workers by white workers].They may modify it, but the condition will not be very materially changed. The white man will meet the Negro on the same ground and work for the same wages. That much we may as well take for granted, calculate the consequences of, and strive by every means to overcome this falling off in our old-time advantages. . . . We must take in some, if not all, of the wages, turn it into capital, hold it, increase it. This must be done as a means of employment for the thousands who cannot get work from old sources. Employment must be had, and this employment will have to come to Negroes from Negro sources. This phase of the Negro's condition is so easily seen that it needs no further consideration. Negro capital will have to give an opportunity to Negro workmen who will be crowded out by white competition; and when I say Negro workmen I would include both sexes. . . . Employment for colored men and women, colored boys and girls must be supplied by colored people. . . .

We are living among the so-called Anglo-Saxons and dealing with them. They are a conquering people who turn their conquests into their pockets. . . . Business seems to be not simply the raw material of Anglo-Saxon civilization—and by business I mean those efforts directly or indirectly concerned with a purposive tendency to material development and progress, with the point in view of the effort bringing material profit or advantage to the one making the effort; and I would include all such efforts whether made in peace or war. I was saying, business seems to be not only simply the raw material of Anglo-Saxon civilization, but almost the civilization itself. It is at least its mainspring to action. Living among such a people is it not obvious that we cannot escape its most powerful motive and survive? To the finite vision, to say the least, the policy of avoiding entrance in the world's business would be suicide to the Negro. Yet as a matter of great account, we ought to note that as good a showing as we have made, that showing is but as pebbles on the shore of business enterprise. . . .[2]

Among the resolutions adopted at the conference was the following:

The mass of the Negroes must learn to patronize business enterprises conducted by their own race, even at some slight disadvantage. We must co-operate or we are lost. Ten million people who join in intelligent self-help can never be long ignored or mistreated.[3]

## 2. The Myth Becomes Institutionalized

Two years after the Atlanta Conference on the Negro in business, Booker T. Washington took the initiative in organizing the National Negro Business League, which held its first meeting in Boston, Massachusetts.[4] At this meeting, attended by 115 delegates from 20 states (mostly southern) and the District of Columbia, Washington was elected president of the permanent organization. The four sessions of the two-day meeting were characterized by much oratory and enthusiasm. In his opening address, Washington made the highly dubious generalization that wherever he had "seen a black man who was succeeding in business, who was a taxpayer, and who possessed intelligence and high character, that individual was treated with the highest respect by the members of the white race."[5] Faith in the power of business enterprise and money to wipe out racial prejudice was repeatedly echoed by the delegates, one of whom stated, "Fortunately human selfishness, the desire of every man to get all he can with least effort or money, has banished all prejudice."[6] These sentiments, it might be noted, won the approval of the leading Boston (white) daily paper.[7]

By far, most of the oratory at this meeting was devoted to the achievements of the Negro in business and the bright future for the Negro in the field of business enterprise. At one point during the meeting, the compiler or statistician interrupted the oratory to announce that according to information provided by the delegates they owned personal and real property amounting to $781,900.[8] In the enthusiasm of the meeting, it appears that no one stopped to realize that even if the figures were true, they represented a very small amount of wealth for 115 businessmen. Nor does it seem that anyone gave sober thought to the report which was presented on the character of Negro business and the amount of capital which it represented.

The report included the study presented at the Atlanta Conference[9] according to which 432 of the 1906 Negro businessmen who sent in reports had small grocery stores; 166 were general merchandise dealers; 162 barbers with $500.00 or more invested in their businesses; 80 undertakers; 68 owners of saloons; 64 had drugstores; and 61 restaurants. The study presented a fair idea of the character of Negro business, since the figures from the United States Census gave a similar picture. These 1906 Negro businessmen represented about a tenth of all persons reported in the Census who, by the broad definition given to "business" by the National Negro Business League, were regarded as engaged in business. For example, the League counted as Negro businessmen the "boarding and lodging house keepers," "hucksters and peddlers," and "newsboys" reported in the Census.

But what else could be expected in a meeting which was

designed to bolster faith in a myth? The delegates were urged to spread the faith in this myth in organizing local business leagues throughout the country.

## 3. Propagation of the Myth

The success of the exhortation to spread the faith in salvation by business is indicated by the fact that within five years more than 300 local business leagues were organized.[10] Then in 1907 there appeared a book on Negro business by Booker T. Washington, who was elected year after year president of the National Business League.[11] This book, which according to the author was written to "take note of the undoubted business awakening among the Negro people of the United States," contained a series of success stories concerning Negroes in various enterprises. The series begins with stories showing how "the Negro farmer often passes from agriculture into business." Outstanding among these farmers who had become businessmen was a Negro farmer from Kansas who became known as "the Negro Potato King." There followed stories of Negroes who had succeeded as caterers, hotel keepers, undertakers, publishers and bankers. One of the leading bankers was a minister whose success, according to Washington, showed "how closely the moral and spiritual interests of our people are interwoven with their material and economical welfare."[12]

It was not strange that a minister was named among the successful Negro businessmen, since the membership of the League was composed largely of professional Negroes, many of whom could hardly have been regarded as businessmen. If one examines the list of members of the Leagues, especially those holding the offices, it will be found that they represent the leadership of the Negroes without respect to their relation to business enterprise. In fact, the report of the Eleventh Annual Conference of the League, which was held in New York City in 1910, stated as one of the notable features of this convention that a "diversity of interests" was represented.[13] Stated otherwise, it was notable in the sense that the crusade to gain supporters for the faith in business enterprise as the salvation of the Negro was gaining adherents among Negroes in all walks of life. The religious nature of this crusade was indicated in the annual address by Booker T. Washington which was delivered in the form of a "Business Sermon" based upon the Biblical text, "To him that hath shall be given."[14] According to Washington, "these lines spoken by the Master strike the keynote for individual success and equally so for racial success." He exhorted his hearers to go out from the meeting "determined that each individual shall be a missionary in his community—a missionary in teaching the masses to get property, to be more thrifty, more economical, and resolve to establish an industrial enterprise wherever a possibility presents itself."[15]

In this same annual address, Washington also stated that "before the starting of the Business League, there was not a single Negro bank in the State of Mississippi. At the present time, Mississippi has eleven Negro banks. When this Business League was organized in Boston ten years ago there were only four Negro banks in the United States; at the present time there are fifty-six Negro banks."[16] If Washington were living today he would probably be saddened by the fact that there are no Negro banks in the State of Mississippi and that there are only eleven Negro banks in the United States, with total assets amounting to less than a single white bank in many small cities.[17] But at the time that the myth of Negro business was being propagated, little concern was shown for the real economic position of the Negro and his experience in business. At each annual meeting of the League, the delegates were exhorted to spread the faith in business enterprise and were told of the golden opportunities to reap wealth by supplying the needs of the Negro masses. At the thirteenth annual convention in Chicago in 1912, Washington asked in his annual address, "If the white man can secure wealth and happiness by owning and operating a coal mine, brick yard, or lime kiln, why can not more Negroes do the same thing? If other races can attain prosperity by securing riches on a large scale from our seas, lakes and rivers in the form of fish and other sea foods, thousands of Negroes can do the same thing. Activity in all these directions finds no races or color line."[18]

Two years later, when the League met in Muskogee, Oklahoma, Washington stated that "when the 2,000,000 Negroes in the Southwest have made the most of their opportunities . . . and brought up the riches contained in the earth they will be able to support . . . 1,000 more grocery stores owned by Negroes, 500 additional dry goods stores, 300 more shoe stores, 200 more good restaurants and hotels, 300 additional millinery stores, 200 additional drug stores and 40 more banks."[19] These fantastic dreams of business enterprise were applauded by the delegates who attended the annual meetings. Moreover, the delegates themselves engaged in oratory about the progress of the black bourgeoisie in obtaining wealth. They related stories of the acquisition of wealth in business enterprises which, when coldly studied, were really of little significance. Nevertheless, the crusade to win believers in the myth of Negro business continued after these conventions closed. It was preached during the pilgrimages which Washington made through the South.[20] During these pilgrimages he constantly pointed out to the Negroes the opportunities which they were overlooking for gaining wealth through business enterprises and he invited Negro businessmen to give testimonies of their achievements in gaining wealth.

After the death of Washington the League continued to carry on the crusade to instill in Negroes faith in business enterprise as the way to economic salvation. Under the influence of the enthusiasm and oratory which characterized these meetings, the participants continued to relate all sorts of fanciful stories concerning their wealth. Myths grew up concerning Negro millionaires that had no basis in fact. The participants, who were drawn from many fields of professional activities, were often led to describe their activities as being inspired by the spirit of business enterprise. For example, at the meeting in Chattanooga, Tennessee, in 1917, Eugene K. Jones, the executive secretary of the National League on Urban Conditions of Negroes, a social work agency, declared that his organization was "a business organization" which made "a business of social welfare work."[21]

While the myth of Negro business was being propagated, the hard realities of the Negro's insignificant achievements in business were apparent to anyone who was not under the spell of the oratory of the conventions of the League. In order to create a substantial basis for the myth, the National Negro Business League undertook to establish the Colored Merchants Association (CMA) grocery stores throughout the country.[22] According to the CMA plan ten or more Negro retail stores in any city were to buy a share of stock in the CMA in which they paid weekly dues and buy from a wholesale dealer selected by the League. The first CMA organization was established in Montgomery, Alabama, in 1928, and soon thereafter organizations were set up in about eighteen other cities. The organization of the CMA was hailed as a new and realistic approach of the League to the promotion of business enterprise among Negroes. *The Chicago Whip*, a Negro newspaper, stated that the establishment of the CMA stores marked the end of the period of oratory and added, "It is well known now that flamboyant oratory makes no lasting impression, gives no deep insight into the manner in which things are done, nor does it convey the information that the untrained business man is so badly in need of."[23] The establishment of the CMA stores was marked by much fanfare. In Harlem, in New York City, the opening of the CMA stores was celebrated by a parade which included men and women from business, fraternal and church circles. Despite the fanfare and hopes of the bourgeoisie, the CMA movement failed after a few years. Those who had bought stock in the CMA lost their money, if not their faith in Negro business enterprise. Those who maintained their faith are still not sure whether the failure was due to the lack of support by Negro retailers or that Negro consumers preferred nationally advertised products.[24]

The failure of the CMA adventure did not affect the faith of the black bourgeoisie in the myth of Negro business, since the faith was constantly being strengthened by the expansion of business education among Negro colleges.[25]

The number of Negro colleges giving business education grew from six in 1900 to more than twenty in 1940. The majority of the students pursuing courses in business receive a technical education in such subjects as typewriting, bookkeeping, and shorthand. In five of the Negro colleges the students are given professional courses in management and other functions exercised by the owners and officials in business enterprises. A small number are prepared to teach the business courses which they have studied. Of the thirty-five graduates of Atlanta University who received the master's degree in business, five were teaching business and eight were employed in Negro colleges as treasurers, business managers, bursars, and one as a registrar.[26] Although twenty-nine of the thirty-five were employed in fields related to the business courses which they had taken, it does not appear that business education had enabled them to become entrepreneurs. The vast majority of students who take technical and business courses in Negro colleges could acquire the same technical competence in some commercial business school. But in the Negro college, business education is given professional status and is glorified because of the myth of Negro business as a way to economic salvation for the Negro in American society.

Beliefs in regard to the myths surrounding Negro business are not affected by the facts presented in Chapter II. For example, it has always been claimed that despite the oppression of the Negro in the South, there was a compensatory fact, namely, that the South offered an opportunity for the development of Negro business. This claim is still made today by those who believe in the myth despite the fact that in proportion to population there are more retail stores in the North than in the South, and that the stores in the North have a larger number of full-time employees and a greater volume of sales. Moreover, despite the fact that there are less than half as many stores in the North as in the South, the total payroll in the North is greater than in the South and the sales three-fourths as great as in the South. Nor has the belief in the myth been affected by the fact that the attempts of Negro businessmen to establish industrial undertakings have constantly resulted in failures. Even when they have had the support of northern white philanthropists, Negroes have failed to establish industries of any importance. For example, during the first decade of the present century, Julius Rosenwald was persuaded by Booker T. Washington to invest $30,000 in a cotton oil mill in Mound Bayou, an all-Negro town in Mississippi. This venture failed, as other such business ventures, and the oil mill was converted into a dance hall.[27] Negroes appealed again to Julius Rosenwald in the 1920's to salvage the wreckage of the manifold undertakings of a Negro banker in Atlanta who attempted to build up a large financial empire on the basis of stores and real estate holdings. But on this occasion, Rosenwald evidently did not think that his philanthropic contributions to Negroes should include the salvaging of their unsound business undertakings.

Nevertheless, northern philanthropy has been sympathetic to the efforts of Negroes to create business enterprises. This has been manifested especially in their financial support of the study of Negro business. Despite the myths surrounding the importance of Negro business, the obvious fact that Negro businesses have failed to become important has continually haunted the minds of the most ardent believers in Negro business as a solution of the Negro's problems. Hence, there has been a constant interest in discovering why Negro businesses have failed so often or have not become important in the economic life of the Negro. A quarter of a century ago, the Spelman Fund, established through Rockefeller contributions to social research, made an initial grant of $15,000, which was supplemented by $5,000, for the study of Negro business. The chief results of this study, which comprised less than fifty pages, were to show that almost all Negro businesses were small retail businesses and undertaking establishments serving Negroes, that they were conducted by their owners, and that they were in Negro neighborhoods. Once again, in 1943, the General Education Board was requested by Atlanta University and the National Urban League to contribute $25,000 to a study of Negro business. The co-operation of the National Urban League was sought by Atlanta University because the League had "become convinced that Negroes might help themselves by improving and expanding the business enterprises which they control."[28]

Neither of these studies revealed the fundamental causes of the failure of Negroes to carry on successful business enterprises either on a small or large scale. They did not deal with the simple but fundamental sociological fact that the Negro lacks a business tradition or the experience of people who, over generations, have engaged in buying and selling. Neither the tradition of the gentleman nor his peasant heritage had provided the Negro with this outlook on the world. Nor did these studies deal with the relation of the efforts of Negroes to establish factories and business enterprises to the structure of the American economy. To have presented such facts these studies would have tended to destroy the Negro's faith in the myth. I have heard Professor Harris criticized by the president of a Negro college because in his book, *The Negro as Capitalist*, he showed that one of the fundamental causes of the failure of Negro banks was the impossibility of the Negro banks to function in a segregated Negro economy which lacked sound businesses requiring credit. The college president's criticism was not directed against the facts presented in this study but against its effect upon the Negro's faith in business enterprise as a solution to his economic problems. The myth concerning Negro business, from the standpoint of many Negro leaders, is more important than the facts of American economic life which determine the fate of Negro business enterprises.

The myth of Negro business is tied up with the belief in the possibility of a separate Negro economy. It has constantly been proposed by those who believe in a separate Negro economy that the Negro can build his own manufacturing plants, stores, and banks with the earnings of Negro workers who, by patronizing these Negro enterprises would create more capital and give employment to Negroes. Of course, behind the idea of the separate Negro economy is the hope of the black bourgeoisie that they will have the monopoly of the Negro market.

They state that it is a sacred obligation of Negroes to patronize Negro business and that they should not complain if they pay higher prices for goods and can not buy exactly what they want so long as they buy from Negroes. During the Depression years, the black bourgeoisie in northern cities began to sponsor a campaign with the slogan, "Don't Buy Where You Can't Work." The result of this campaign was the growth of anti-Semitism which expressed itself during race riots when Jewish businessmen in Negro neighborhoods became the targets of Negro mobs.[29]

The idea of a separate Negro economy was given an odd turn by a Negro college professor who taught and popularized the theory of the "double duty" dollar.[30] According to this theory, the Negro worker would not only purchase with his dollar the necessities of life, but he would provide with the dollar he spent the wages for Negro workers. Anyone who opposed this fanciful economic theory was called an enemy of Negroes. As the result of the faith in the myth of Negro business there have sprung up all over the country fanciful schemes, such as one recently started in the national capital which proposed that each Negro, man, woman and child contribute one dollar to a fund to establish manufacturing plants which would make shoes and clothes for the Negro market.

## 4. The Myth and the Changing Status of the Negro

The changing status of the Negro in the United States, which has resulted from World War II and the world crisis, has not failed to influence the myth of Negro business. Paradoxically, on the surface at least, the increasing employment of Negroes desiring business careers by white business enterprises has not shaken faith in the myth of Negro business. The reason for this becomes apparent when one considers the relation of the myth to the world of make-believe which the black bourgeoisie has created.

As we have seen, the black bourgeoisie derives its income almost entirely from white-collar and professional occupations which give it a privileged status within the isolated Negro community. Since the black bourgeoisie has rejected identification with the masses, its isolation has been further intensified. In escaping from identification with the masses, the black bourgeoisie has attempted to identify with the white propertied classes. Since this has been impossible, except in their minds, because of the racial barriers those identified with this class have attempted to act out their role in a world of make-believe. In the world of make-believe they have not taken over the patterns of behavior of the white-collar and professional white workers, but the values and as far as possible the patterns of behavior of wealthy whites. With their small earnings, their attempt to maintain the style of living of the white propertied classes has only emphasized the unreality of their way of life. Faith in the myth of Negro business, which symbolizes the power and status of white America, has been the main element in the world of make-believe that the black bourgeoisie has created.

The prosperity which the United States enjoyed as the result of World War II and the war economy during the Cold War has trickled down to the Negroes, especially since some of the barriers to the employment of Negroes have been lowered. The increase in the earnings of Negro workers has brought increased prosperity to Negro businesses, especially to Negro insurance companies and the Negro publishers of newspapers and magazines. Also, the lowering of barriers to the employment of Negroes in white-collar occupations has increased the proportion of Negroes able to maintain a middle-class standard of life. Despite these improvements in the position of the black bourgeoisie, there were some misgivings about the continuance of their prosperous condition after the War. The feeling that it was necessary to assess the economic improvement in the condition of Negroes in white-collar and professional occupations was the chief motivation for calling a conference at Howard University in 1946.[31]

At the opening session of this conference, the president of Howard University declared that,

> The Negro people, just a bit over eighty years from slavery, are a child people in their ability to organize the

ordinary things that have to do with effective existence. Take the simple things that engage the attention of a community and involve the major activities of human beings in a small town—the gathering together and the distribution of food in a grocery store, a butcher shop, or a restaurant. In the little one-horse town or your Harlem or your Los Angeles, you miss Negro faces in this fundamental business of assembling and distributing food products. We have a handful of men engaged in the grocery business, a handful in the butcher business, and a handful in the bakery business—although we have some of the best bread bakers in the world. We have nobody in the pastry business. There is also the question of clothing. Any group of 10,000 human beings will naturally require a certain amount of clothing of all kinds. Go into the communities where we live. Enterprises and persons engaged in the effective distribution of these things—to say nothing of their production—are practically missing among us. Then there are some of the service activities connected with clothing—for example, the laundry business. There are practically no Negro-operated laundries, even in the Southern area, where we used to monopolize the washing of clothes. We have so few tailor shops or millinery shops. Yet none of these things are beyond our power. We just simply have not focused our attention upon them.[32]

Much of the discussion at this conference was of the same nature, dealing with the failure of the Negro to seize the opportunity to organize businesses which would thrive on the Negro market. Scarcely any attention was given to the organization of American economic life and how this fact affected the prospects of Negro business. Nor was any discussion directed to the fact that Negro white-collar and professional workers could not assemble the capital and organize the managerial ability necessary for large-scale production and distribution. There was in this conference, as in the conferences of the National Negro Business League, much exhortation to Negroes to engage in business, which revealed a continued faith in the myth of Negro business as providing a solution to the economic problems of the Negro.

When the National Business League celebrated its fiftieth anniversary in 1950 at Tuskegee Institute, the League rededicated itself to the achievement of the aims of the founder. Booker T. Washington. The president of the League announced that the philosophy upon which the League was founded was "as potent today as it was when it was first given. From the very beginning of the League," he added, "its preachments, propaganda and programs have been directed towards alerting our minds to the importance of entering into and building business of all kinds and to the necessity of becoming business minded on a national scale."[33] However, only two years later, when the president of the League reported on the results of his attempt, during his travels amounting to 172,000 miles, to develop faith in the importance and future of Negro business, he had to meet the objection that the League's program really provided for a separate economy. The president said that it did not take him long to convince the person who raised the objection "that a separate economy was a myth." Then he explained, "The customer of the Negro-owned grocery may work for and get his money from employment at General Motors— or General Electric, or at the Ford Automobile Plant, or in department stores owned by other groups—that fact alone eliminates the possibility of a separate economy."[34] Then the president attempted to show how other minority groups, especially the Jews, had become important in the economic life of various countries through their separate business operations.

That the president of the National Negro Business League felt that it was necessary to repudiate the myth of a separate economy, while defending the myth of Negro business, was due to the fact that Negroes were beginning to secure employment on an unprecedented scale in the marketing branches of white businesses. White firms have found it extremely profitable to employ Negroes in advertising products for Negro consumers, in establishing public relations with the Negro community, and as salesmen. Negroes have been employed on a large scale by the distributors of liquors, beers and non-alcoholic beverages, cigarettes, gasoline and automobiles. The employment of Negroes by large corporations has overshadowed even the exaggerated achievements of Negro businessmen. The importance of the employment of aspiring Negro businessmen in white enterprises stimulated the department of Business Administration at Howard University to hold a "Career Conference in Marketing" in February, 1954. At this conference, the new careers which were opening up to Negroes were discussed and the successful examples of Negroes in these new occupations were presented to students who wanted to become businessmen.

The employment of Negroes in the field of marketing or distribution by large American corporations is a phase of the integration of the Negro into American life. The National Negro Business League, which has proclaimed since its establishment that business success would break down racial barriers, has been compelled to go along with this new development. In fact, some of the younger members of the National Business League, many of whom are not really engaged in *Negro* business, have proposed to delete "Negro" from the name of the League. But this has not met with general acceptance because the leaders recognize that "integration" means the ultimate disappearance of *Negro* business. Some Negro businessmen have pointed to cities where Negroes have recently been accepted into "white" restaurants, theaters, and cinemas to show how integration has meant the decline in *Negro* business. Moreover, as the increasing economic welfare of the Negro has produced all sorts of extravagant claims about the purchasing power of Negroes, Negro businessmen have sought a share in this market.[35]

The myth of Negro business has also been strengthened by the encouragement which the white community has given to the belief of Negroes that the accumulation of wealth through business will solve their problems. Negro salesmen, who are employed by white business and are only sentimentally attached to *Negro* business, are meeting at luncheons with white salesmen; and Negro salesmen are being featured in the public relations literature sent out by corporations. Yet no Negro businessmen are taken into the white business groups which own and control the life of the American community. The white community is assured, nevertheless, that the Negro leaders who propagate the myth of Negro business are uncompromising enemies of any radical doctrines. The myth that Negroes were spending 15 billion dollars in 1951 was widely circulated by whites as well as Negroes since it served to exaggerate the economic well-being of Negroes in the United States and to whet the appetites of the black bourgeoisie, both *Negro* businessmen and Negroes employed by American corporations, in their efforts to reap benefits from the increased earnings of Negroes.

The myth of Negro business thrives despite the fact that Negro businessmen can best be described as a "lumpen-bourgeoisie."[36] The myth of Negro business is fed by the false notions and values that are current in the isolated social world of the Negro, a world dominated by the views and mental outlook of the black bourgeoisie. The extent to which these false notions influence the outlook of Negroes cannot better be illustrated than by the case of the Negro Pullman porter who owned his home and four shares of stock, valued at about eighty dollars, in a large American corporation. He declared that he was against the policies of Franklin D. Roosevelt and the New Deal because they taxed men of property like himself in order to assist lazy working men. Such delusions are created largely, as we shall see in the next chapter, by the Negro press.

# Chapter VIII

## The Negro Press and Wish-Fulfillment

THE NEGRO PRESS is not only one of the most successful business enterprises owned and controlled by Negroes; it is the chief medium of communication which creates and perpetuates the world of make-believe for the black bourgeoisie. Although the Negro press declares itself to be the spokesman for the Negro group as a whole, it represents essentially the interests and outlook of the black bourgeoisie. Its demand for equality for the Negro in American life is concerned primarily with opportunities which will benefit the black bourgeoisie economically and enhance the social status of the Negro. The Negro press reveals the inferiority complex of the black bourgeoisie and provides a documentation of the attempts of this class to seek compensations for its hurt self-esteem and exclusion from American life. Its exaggerations concerning the economic well-being and cultural achievements of Negroes, its emphasis upon Negro "society" all tend to create a world of make-believe into which the black bourgeoisie can escape from its inferiority and inconsequence in American society.

### 1. The Romance of Urban Life

The Negro press, like the press of other ethnic and racial minorities in American life, began as a medium for the expression of the opinions of the small intelligentsia among Negroes. The first Negro paper, *Freedom's Journal,* was established in 1827 by two free Negroes, one of whom, John Russworm, was the first Negro to be graduated from an American college.[1] Twenty years later appeared the *North Star,* the name of which was changed later to *Frederick Douglass's Paper.* These papers were concerned primarily with the abolition of slavery and with protest against the civil discriminations against Negroes. After the Civil War a number of Negro newspapers came into existence, especially after 1880, as the Negro migrated to cities.[2] At the opening of the present century, the two most important Negro newspapers were the *Guardian* and the *New York Age*. The *Guardian*, published in Boston by Monroe Trotter, a distinguished graduate of Harvard, expressed the militant demands of Negro intellectuals for Negro equality, while the *New York Age* became the principal mouthpiece for the program of Booker T. Washington.

A new period in the history of Negro newspapers was inaugurated by Robert Abbott, who had started the (Chicago) *Defender* in 1905 as a mere handbill. In 1910 Abbott employed an assistant who began to use headlines, containing sensational news, in order to attract attention. This represented a departure from the traditional type of Negro newspaper that had been designed to attract the Negro intelligentsia. Although this device tended to increase the sale of the (Chicago) *Defender*, it was the mass migrations from the South during and following the first World War that caused the (Chicago) *Defender* to become the leading Negro newspaper and to exceed 100,000 circulation by 1922. During and following the first World War, the (Chicago) *Defender* became the most important medium for stimulating migration of Negroes from the South. In the *Defender* the North was represented as a Promised Land to which the oppressed Negro could escape. Thousands of letters were sent by Negroes in the South to the *Defender*, asking for help in order to move to the North where they could find an opportunity for employment for themselves and educational opportunities for their children.[3] At the same time the *Defender* became the defender of the rights of the Negro, exposing discriminations against Negroes in the North and protesting against lynching and other forms of oppression of the Negro in the South. The spectacular success of the *Defender* was due to the fact that it provided for the mental stimulation which the Negroes experienced in the urban environment. For the masses of Negroes who had escaped from the social and mental isolation of the rural South, the northern metropolis opened a new world of ideas and adventure. The Negro's imagination was awakened by the marvels of the city, which offered various escapes from the pent-up existence which he had known. The northern city provided mental stimulation not only for the Negro folk, but for the educated Negro as well. It was during and immediately following the first World War that the *Messenger*, a magazine advocating socialist ideas, was established and became popular. Likewise, during this period, the *Crisis*, the official publication of the National Association for the Advancement of Colored People, became, under the editorship of W. E. B. DuBois, the most important magazine of public opinion among Negroes.[4]

Between the first World War and World War II, the number and circulation of Negro newspapers grew rapidly because of the continued urbanization of the Negro and the increase in literacy among them. More than two-thirds of the Negro newspapers which were in existence in 1943 had been established after the close of the first World War.[5] In 1943 there were 164 active newspapers, 58 of which were published in 20 cities which had 50,000 or more Negro inhabitants in 1940. Of the 144 Negro newspapers on which information was provided, 114 were published regularly each week and had a combined average circulation per issue of more than 1,600,000 copies. Although about two-thirds of the papers were published in the South, the most important Negro newspapers from the standpoint of circulation and influence were and still are published in northern cities.

World War II acclerated the growth and importance of Negro newspapers. During the War four Negro newspapers emerged as the most important organs of opinion among Negroes: the *Pittsburgh Courier* with a weekly circulation of about 270,000; the *Afro-American* (Baltimore, Maryland), with a circulation of about 230,000; the (Chicago) *Defender* with about 160,000; and the *Journal and Guide* (Norfolk, Virginia) with around 78,000. All of these papers, like most Negro newspapers (with the single exception of a small daily paper published in Atlanta, Georgia) began as weekly publications. In order to provide more up-to-date news, the *Pittsburgh Courier* and the *Afro-American* have instituted two weekly editions. They have reached other Negro communities and increased their circulation by publishing special editions in four or five cities. The *Defender*, which became a daily in 1956, has a special national edition that circulates throughout the country, while the *Journal and Guide*, the most important Negro newspaper published in the South, has a national edition that is read on the eastern seaboard. As the circulation of Negro newspapers has grown, news-gathering agencies have come into existence, the most important of which is the Associated Negro Press, established in 1919.

The Negro newspaper came into existence as an organ of the "Negro protest"[6] and it grew in importance because the white press ignored what was considered "news" in the Negro community. Moreover, since Negroes read white newspapers, if the same news is published in Negro newspapers it must have a special "slant" in order to appeal to Negroes. Therefore, the Negro newspaper not only reports what happens in the isolated Negro social world, but presents the events in the larger world in a manner which has meaning for Negroes in their isolated social existence. Since the Negro newspaper makes its appeal to the awakened imagination of Negroes in urban communities, it provides a romantic escape for Negro city-dwellers. During World War II, a number of Negro magazines, similar to *Life*, with pictures accompanied by romantic stories of the activities of Negroes, both inside and outside of the United States, began to circulate widely among Negroes. The most important of these magazines, *Ebony*, *Jet*, *Hue*, and *Tan Confessions*, the last renamed *Tan* and made a full-sized magazine, are published by the same company. While *Ebony* deals especially with the achievements and personal lives of Negroes who are public figures, *Jet* contains gossip concerning personalities in Negro life. Although *Tan* is not as sensational as its predecessor, it nevertheless carries stories of sex attraction and romantic love both sanctioned and condemned by the prevailing mores. *Hue*, a pocket-sized magazine like *Jet*, carries general news of the Negro world and tends to romanticize the everyday activities of Negroes. Although the

Negro press, including magazines as well as newspapers, claims to be published in the interest of the "race" (the Negro), it represents primarily the interests of the black bourgeoisie and promulgates the bourgeois values of the make-believe world of the black bourgeoisie.

## 2. Achievements of the "Race"

Since the Negro press has always claimed that one of its functions was to present to the world a proper picture of the Negro, it has naturally placed much emphasis upon the achievements of Negroes. However, the reports which the Negro press has given concerning Negro achievements are primarily an attempt to compensate for the collective inferiority of the Negro, especially of the black bourgeoisie. Consequently, the significance which the Negro press attributes to these achievements generally has little relation to the world of reality outside of the world of make-believe into which the black bourgeoisie has found an escape. In the past the achievements reported by the Negro press were concerned mostly with some distinctions which Negroes achieved in the field of education, literature, music, the theatre, politics, and sports. Then, too, much emphasis was placed upon the role of Negroes in American history. Negro newspapers have not restricted, however, their accounts of the achievements of the Negro to the United States. The literary accomplishments of the Dumas' in France and of Pushkin in Russia are constantly presented to Negroes. Even obscure and relatively unknown persons of Negro descent are represented to the Negro public as persons who have played important roles in history. Recently, for example, Samuel Johnson's Negro servant, who was painted by Sir Joshua Reynolds, was featured as an example of the Negro in the world of art.[7] Sometimes historical figures whose features or dark complexion can be made the basis of a claim that they are of Negroid ancestry are presented as evidence of the importance of the Negro in history.

But it is more often the petty achievements of living Negroes that are reported as if they were of great importance. The appointments of Negroes to minor positions in the federal and state governments are reported as great achievements. In the Negro press mere police magistrates become judges. As the result of the exaggeration of the achievements of Negroes, myths grow up about the accomplishments of Negroes. Myths grow up concerning the importance of books written by Negroes. A Negro student who makes a good record in a northern university may be reported to be a genius. The awarding of a doctorate to a Negro by a northern university is still reported as if it had great significance. One myth which has appeared in Negro newspapers concerns a Negro who knows so much about his subject that no university in the world has a faculty with sufficient knowledge to award him a doctorate.[8] Since the Negro has begun to travel abroad, myths have grown up in regard to the artistic and intellectual achievements of Negroes in foreign countries. These myths, which help to create the world of make-believe for the Negro, will be discussed in the section dealing with the recognitions accorded the Negro.

As the black bourgeoisie has grown in importance in the Negro community during the past two decades, the Negro press has focused attention upon activities of the Negro in business and his achievements in acquiring wealth. In a newspaper which devotes nearly half a page to business, it is reported that the Citizens Trust Company, a Negro bank in Atlanta, has petitioned the Georgia Secretary of State to permit it to amend its charter in order to raise its capital stock from $200,000 to $300,000.[9] Along with this announcement appears another news item, stating that a senior student in the Negro State College in Petersburg, Virginia, was the winner of the *Wall Street Journal* Students Award for 1954.[10] Three weeks earlier there appeared in this same paper the announcement that a Greek letter sorority in Nashville, Tennessee, was planning for its National Business Week.[11] In a news story with a picture of the ceremony, this paper reported three weeks later that the wife of the president of the Negro college in the same city crowned an employee of a Negro church publishing house "Miss Business and Professional."[12] In the business column of this same paper, one learns that a business fraternity is being organized in the Negro State College in Greensboro, North Carolina. However, these typical items which were taken at random from the business column of a Negro newspaper lack the romance that surrounds the Negro's acquisition of wealth which one finds in *Ebony*.

Five years ago, *Ebony* carried an editorial entitled "Time to Stop Begging."[13] The editorial opened with the sentence, "In this day of confiscatory income taxes, all-powerful labor unions, and fast-spending heiresses, dusk seems to be approaching for the American age of philanthropy." As a result, according to the editorial, Negroes can not look to philanthropy for the "bountiful benevolence" which supported their institutions. Fortunately, however, this will bring an end to the control which philanthropy once exercised over Negro leaders, a pattern which had been set by Booker T. Washington. Then the editorial asks the question, "Where Is the Money Coming from?" (to support Negro institutions). It answers this question by saying that it will come from Negroes. Then it informs its readers that there are at least a dozen Negro millionaires and that the total income of Negroes exceeds $10 billion.

In this same issue there is an illustrated article on "The Ten Richest Negroes in America." The ten richest Negroes included an eighty-two-year-old retired "multi-millionaire" in Texas; the head of the North Carolina Mutual Life Insurance Company and a number of businesses in Durham, North Carolina; the wealthiest Negro undertaker; Marian Anderson; two brothers, "multi-millionaires," who were kings of the "policy racket"; two brothers who own cotton farms and manufactured embalming fluid; a specialist who is considered the richest Negro doctor; Father Divine; two brothers who acquired wealth from oil on their farm in Oklahoma; and a Jamaica-born Negro who owns real estate in New York City. The article informs the reader that the Negro capitalist in Durham has a $25,000 home and draws an annual salary of $20,000, while the undertaker has an annual income of $100,000. The Negro doctor has an eighteen-room house in Chicago valued at $45,000, while the owners of the oil wells in Oklahoma have received as much as $25,000 monthly from the three big corporations to which they leased their oil wells.

The reader is also informed that one of the brothers who owned the oil wells once owned a $6,500 custom-built Chrysler Thunderbolt, while the other brother gave his divorced wife a $50,000 home, an automobile, and $400 a month for life. It did not mention how his divorced wife would maintain a $50,000 home and an automobile on $400 a month.

Accompanying the story of each of the six of the richest Negroes in America there is information on the next richest Negro. For example, the reader learns that the next richest Negro doctor has an annual income of $25,000 and has a home worth $40,000. Next to Marian Anderson is a Negro comedian who earns $150,000 annually and owns a home worth $50,000; and next to Father Divine is a leader of a cult, Elder Solomon Lightfoot Micheaux, who has gained notoriety as the "Happy Am I" radio preacher. Second to the two kings of the "policy racket," who are supposed to be worth $3,000,000, is a policy king who is worth $500,000 and owns a suburban home valued at $25,000.

A later issue of *Ebony* of the same year contained an illustrated article entitled "Wealthy Widows."[14] In the introduction to this article, it was stated that "Along with white society, Negro America too has its share of widows of both kinds—'the merry widows' and the retiring old-in-years-and-in-spirit variety." Leading the list of wealthy "society" widows is the widow of the king of the "policy racket" in Chicago. In addition to a $150,000 trust fund, the dead "policy king" left his widow $30,000 in American Telephone and Telegraph stocks. Then follow pictures and stories of twenty-five other wealthy widows. Five of these widows inherited their money from husbands who were undertakers, five from real estate dealers, and five from physicians. There were two widows who owed their money to husbands who were newspaper men and two whose husbands were in the life insurance business. The remaining six widows were the beneficiaries of husbands who were, respectively, a night club owner, a police magistrate, an officer in a fraternal organization, a dentist, a "policy king," and the owner of a trucking business. The reader learns that the widow of one undertaker has an annual income above $20,-000; that she follows the races, and drove to the Kentucky Derby in one of her Cadillacs; and that she "sports diamonds and expensive clothes." Similar details are presented on the wealth, tastes, and habits of other wealthy widows.

Hardly a month passes that *Ebony* does not carry a story in its section devoted to "Business" concerning the success of Negroes in acquiring wealth. In the December, 1948 issue there was, for example, the story of a former Negro teacher of economics in a southern Negro college accompanied by a picture of him in front of his office which, the reader is informed, is near Wall Street. This former Negro teacher, who was a soldier in the Philippine Islands during World War II, had acquired a fortune by buying vehicles that had been discarded by the United States Army and selling them after they had been reconditioned. Or, to take a story of a different nature, which was intended to show the Negro's acquisition of wealth within the Negro group, one may turn to the issue of May, 1953. This illustrated story, which was entitled "Death a Big Business," told how Negro undertakers, or "morticians" as they have come to be known, do a gross business of $120 million a year as the result of 150,000 Negro funerals. According to *Ebony,* the 3,000 Negro undertakers have a monopoly on burying Negroes and their mortuaries have become the most attractive buildings owned by Negroes in most cities. In some of the smaller towns Negro undertakers are not only the richest Negroes, but their businesses constitute the only Negro business.

It appears from the statement of one undertaker that Negroes insist upon having Cadillacs for the funerals of their relatives. Their desire in regard to Cadillacs seems to be a reasonable demand in the light of the editorial which appeared in *Ebony* in September, 1949. In this editorial entitled, "Why Negroes Buy Cadillacs," it was stated that wealthy Negroes should not be criticized any more for buying Cadillacs while the masses of Negroes live in slums than well-to-do whites who buy Cadillacs when numerous whites are unemployed. The editorial concludes that although too often Negroes with Cadillacs can not afford them, the Cadillac is a worthy symbol of their aspiration to be a genuinely first-class American.

In becoming first-class Americans, Negroes (at least the black bourgeoisie) are breaking into the money market of the United States, according to *Ebony*. In an illustrated article entitled "Negroes in Wall Street," there were featured in the October, 1950, issue two young Negroes, each of whom is employed by a brokerage firm in Wall Street. According to the article, these young Negroes are pushing a campaign to lure postwar Negro savings into the investment field. In the same issue there is an illustrated story entitled "Death Comes to the World's Richest Negro," which describes how the Texas multimillionaire, referred to above, was buried. The Texas "multimillionaire" lay in state in a $5,000 satin-finished bronze casket surrounded by more than $2,000 in wreaths and floral designs. In the funeral procession, which was two-and-a-half miles long, there was a succession of Cadillacs including two Cadillac flower-wagons which were specially built. As in the case of many other wealthy Negroes, when this Negro "multimillionaire" died, only $100,000 remained of his reputed $3,000,000 fortune. In addition, however, there were a Young Men's Christian Association building in memory of his son, who died mysteriously while a student at Harvard University, and a $38,000 marker over his grave.

From the stories which appear in *Ebony* it seems that rich Negroes are appearing faster than they are dying. The issue of March, 1954, carried the story of "Who Are the Newly Rich?" According to *Ebony* a group of newly rich Negroes have quietly emerged during the past ten years. They are conservative; they are not ostentatious in their display of wealth, but live comfortably though modestly in $40,000 to $50,000 homes. They are interested in good books and the opera, to which they subscribe, and send their children to the best schools. These newly rich Negroes, according to *Ebony*, represent only a small proportion of the hundreds of rich Negroes who have assets ranging from $100,000 to $1,000,000. Heading the list is Jackie Robinson, the first Negro to play in organized baseball, who has an annual income of $32,000 from baseball and $15,000 from broadcasting. Another of the newly rich Negroes is a woman who has built a million-dollar beauty business. She and a lawyer are shown in a picture accompanying the article, entering the Metropolitan Opera House. The other newly rich Negroes include several who have accumulated fortunes in real estate; a director of a Negro loan and investment company; an owner of a restaurant, hotel, barber shop, drugstore and pool room; an automobile salesman; a paving contractor; a director of a savings and loan association; a nationally known research chemist; a building contractor; and a physician who has large real estate holdings. In fact, the reader is informed in another article in this same issue of *Ebony* that the majority of Negro physicians no longer depend entirely upon their professional work for their incomes.

Although *Our World*, a picture magazine similar in many respects to *Ebony*, does not report to the same extent as the latter the accumulation of wealth by Negroes, a perusal of its pages will show that it does not fail to inform the public of the prosperity of the black bourgeoisie. For example, in the June, 1954 issue, there is the story of the phenomenal rise to prominence of a councilman in a northern city. While the wife of the councilman, the readers are told, thought that he was very sensational in 1935 with a salary of $5,000, the councilman now has a total annual income of more than $20,000. In the issue of October, 1953, the readers are told the story of "Daddy" Grace, a leader of a religious cult, who is described as a "millionaire with a Bible," who built up a "real estate empire." The April, 1953 issue reported the story of the Negro "Men of Distinction" who, as the result of being featured in the ads of a large whiskey distillery, were taken on a hilarious pleasure trip to Florida. This story was an indication of the recognition shown the black bourgeoisie by the white business world.

## 3. Recognition of the "Race"

Because of its deep-seated inferiority complex, the black bourgeoisie hungers for any form of recognition by people or groups that have status or power in the world. The Negro press provides this recognition for the black bourgeoisie in various ways. It plays up any recognition that is accorded American Negroes by any of the so-called independent colored nations. In the past, the subjects of some of these colored nations studiously avoided identification with American Negroes. Nevertheless, when in recent years the subjects of these colored nations showed a disposition to accept American Negroes, the black bourgeoisie seized upon the opportunity to gain recognition. Whenever American Negroes visit Haiti and are accorded any recognition, or whenever Haitians in the United States invite them to their social affairs, the event is featured in the Negro press. Moreover, despite the fact that Ethiopians make it clear that they are not Negroes, the black bourgeoisie seeks every opportunity to gain some recognition from the Emperor of that country. When the Emperor visited the United States recently, the Negro press played up the fact that he consented to receive one of their reporters and had sent a message to American Negroes advising them to continue their social and intellectual advancement with Christian courage.[15]

The Negro press also features any recognition shown Negroes by Liberia. This does not mean, however, that the black bourgeoisie is seeking identification with Africans as a racial group. Because of their ignorance the majority of the black bourgeoisie still regard Africans as savages or exotic people and speak condescendingly of the developments which have occurred in Africa if they happen to hear of them. At the same time the Negro press in its role as the defender of the "race" may give lip service to pride in being a Negro. For example, the Negro press featured a letter written by Jackie Robinson, the black baseball idol, to a Negro orphan, who had been overheard to say that he wished he were white, telling him to be proud that he was a Negro.[16] A mere perusal of Negro newspapers and magazines will reveal that a large part of their income is derived from the advertisements of products which will remove or modify Negroid characteristics. These advertisements tell how the Negro can rid himself of his black or dark complexion, or how he can straighten his hair. It was through the manufacture of such products that Madame Walker, one of the first "rich Negroes" to gain notoriety, made a fortune and set a standard for conspicuous consumption that has become legendary.

While rejecting any genuine identification with the black race, the black bourgeoisie seeks nevertheless whatever recognition it may enjoy because of the high status of individuals of Negro ancestry in the world. Consequently, the Negro press is compelled to focus attention upon the relatively few Negroes who have gained any form of recognition in the white world. The few Negroes who have gained recognition consist chiefly of entertainers and leaders of organizations who have contacts with whites. Dr. Ralph J. Bunche has a unique position in this respect, since not a week passes that the Negro press fails to carry news about him and his achievements. Every recognition that Dr. Bunche has received has been interpreted as a form of recognition for the black bourgeoisie—who have been all the more inclined to identify with him because he is not black. In playing up the recognition which the Negro receives, the Negro press utilizes the most trivial events. A Negro actor needs only to play the most insignificant role, even the role of a servant, in connection with some prominent white actor for the event to be played up as a form of recognition. Sometimes the recognition which is accorded the Negro involves questionable relations with whites. For example, the fact that a white man was found dead in Canada with an American Negro woman in what was described as a "love tryst" was featured on the front page of a Negro paper.[17]

In reporting any recognition which the Negro may receive the Negro press is not concerned with principles or values except where status, in a narrow sense, is concerned. It would be quick to criticize an "Uncle Tom" or a Negro who would suggest that the Negro should not be treated as a citizen with the same rights as white citizens. But the Negro press is not concerned with broader social and economic values. It will give prominence with avowed or unavowed approval to any recognition that is given the Negro by any organization in the United States so long as there is no implication of *racial* inferiority. For example, it featured the election of a Negro doctor to the presidency of a local affiliate of the American Medical Association although this doctor had opposed a national health program which would have benefited the masses of Negroes and had been elected to an office in the American Medical Association, which is opposed to "socialized medicine."[18] Or, to take an example on the international front: the fact that black troops participated in the defense of Dien-Bien-Phu is the only interest that the Negro press has shown in the war in Indo-China.[19] Even when the Negro press shows any interest in the colonial problem, it is generally concerned with the social status and recognition of the black elite in colonial areas.

The lack of interest of the black bourgeoisie and its mouthpiece, the Negro press, in the broader issues facing the modern world is due to the fact that the Negro has developed no economic or social philosophy except the opportunistic philosophy that the black intelligentsia has evolved to justify its anomalous and insecure position. Of course, plain ignorance of the nature of the modern world and the revolution which is in progress accounts also for the outlook of the Negro press. Negro journalists have been recruited on the whole from the inferior, segregated Negro schools, and their outlook has been restricted by the social and mental isolation of the Negro world. Following the example of the white press, the Negro press has its commentators or columnists who discuss current issues for their readers. With a few rare exceptions the columnists who write for the Negro press reveal the limitations of their knowledge of economic and social forces in the modern world. When they would pretend to be sophisticated, they exhibit a smart-alecky or bumptious attitude toward sound knowledge. They are generally careful, however, never to offend the black bourgeoisie nor to challenge white opinion on fundamental economic and political issues. In fact, except in regard to race relations, the columnists generally echo the conservative opinions and platitudes of the white world on crucial issues. For example, one widely read columnist who boasts of "independent" thinking, has constantly asserted that he opposed "the Chinese Republic's shooting its way into the United Nations." By echoing the opinions of the white community the intellectual leaders of the black bourgeoisie hope to secure the approval and recognition of the white propertied classes with whom they seek identification.

In creating a world of make-believe to satisfy the craving of the black bourgeoisie for recognition, the Negro press constantly draws upon the reputed experiences of Negroes in Europe. Since the majority of Negroes, including even those who are educated, still regard Europe as a faraway fabulous land, the reporters for the Negro press can give free rein to their imagination. From time to time the Negro press gives glowing accounts of Negro men and women who have captivated European royalty. Negroes living in humble circumstances on meager incomes are reported often to have richly furnished chateaux which are the meeting place for European intellectuals and people of wealth. In a recent issue of *Ebony*, one reads of a retired Negro customs inspector who has become the playboy of the Riviera and associates with princes and princesses.[20] When Negro entertainers have entertained for wealthy or aristocratic Europeans, it is reported in the Negro press as if they were accepted by European "society." The reports of the performances of Negro artists are generally misrepresentations of their actual accomplishments. There was, for example, the case of the Negro pianist who, according to the Negro press, had been acclaimed by French critics, whereas in fact the critics had said that her performance was on the level of a beginning student. Similar misrepresentations are reported concerning the intellectual achievements of Negroes in Europe. Negroes who scarcely ever attend the lectures at European universities are represented as brilliant students. Not long ago, when a president of a Negro college who could scarcely read French visited Europe, it was reported that he had dazzled the professors in French universities by lecturing in perfect French.

These fanciful reports are provided for the black bourgeoisie who remain at home. The black bourgeoisie, who have always exhibited an intense xenophobia especially where white people are concerned, have avoided traveling abroad because, as one Negro school teacher put it, "No one would know who we are." In recent years, however, the black bourgeoisie have begun to go abroad. Although many of them are school teachers, they do not want to travel as white school teachers because they are members of Negro "society." Therefore, in preparation for their voyage they spend large sums of money on clothes which they will never have occasion to wear. Since they fail to meet European royalty, they generally write home stories of how they impressed Europeans with the money which they spent freely. Nevertheless, the Negro press generally reports their journeys to Europe as conquests of European "society."

As we see, then, the fantastic accounts of the achievements of Negroes and of the recognition accorded them by whites constitute important elements in the world of make-believe which the Negro press has created to compensate for the feelings of inferiority of the black bourgeoisie. But there are still more important elements in the world of unreality in which the black bourgeoisie lives. These consist of the reports on the activities of Negro "society," which form the major part of the news items on individuals in the Negro press. Because of the importance given to Negro "society" and the values which it cherishes, it will be necessary to consider this phase of the world of make-believe separately in the following chapter.

# Chapter IX

## "Society": Status without Substance

THERE IS A PHASE of the world of make-believe of the black bourgeoisie which requires special treatment, namely, the activities of those persons who constitute its "society." Although Negro "society" was not created by the Negro press, it is the Negro press which feeds and perpetuates the illusions of this element in the black bourgeoisie. The activities of "society" are not simply a form of social life engaged in for pleasure and friendly social intercourse. They are engaged in primarily in order to maintain status or as a part of the competition for status. The activities of "society" serve to differentiate the black bourgeoisie from the masses of poorer Negroes and at the same time compensate for the exclusion of the black bourgeoisie from the larger white community. However, the behavior and standards of consumption which are maintained by "society" generally lack the economic base which such activities presuppose. "Society" thus provides one of the main escapes from the world of reality into a world of make-believe.

## 1. Evolution of "Society"

"Society" among Negroes had its roots among the house servants who enjoyed a certain prestige among the other slaves on the plantation during their social gatherings. An ex-slave, who wrote his autobiography after escaping to freedom, has provided a vivid account of the status of this group on a plantation.

It was about ten o'clock when the aristocratic slaves began to assemble, dressed in the cast-off finery of their master and mistress, swelling out and putting on airs in imitation of those they were forced to obey from day to day.

House servants were, of course, "the stars" of the party; all eyes were turned to them to see how they conducted, for they, among slaves, are what a military man would call "fugle-men." The field hands, and such of them as have generally been excluded from the dwelling of their owners, look to the house servants as a pattern of politeness and gentility. And indeed, it is often the only method of obtaining any knowledge of the manners of what is called "genteel society"; hence, they are ever regarded as a privileged class; and are sometimes greatly envied, while others are bitterly hated.[1]

After Emancipation, some of the social distinctions which had grown up among the slaves continued to function. Negroes who were free before the Emancipation Proclamation or who could boast of a distinguished family background set themselves apart from the masses of freedmen and constituted a distinct upper social class. Many of them boasted of their "blood," which generally referred to their white ancestry. A mulatto witness of the history of Negroes during the years following the Civil War has left a rather satirical account of the emergence of "society" among them in the nation's capital.

There is another element in this strange heterogeneous conglomeration, which for want of a better name has been styled society and it is this species of African humanity which is forever and ever informing the uninitiated what a narrow escape they had from being born white. They have small hands, aristocratic insteps and wear blue veins, they have auburn hair and finely chiselled features. They are uneducated as a rule (i.e.) the largest number of them, though it would hardly be discovered unless they opened their *mouths* in the presence of their superiors in intellect, which they are very careful not to do. In personal appearance, they fill the bill precisely so far as *importance* and pomposity goes—but no farther. They are opposed to manual labor, their physical organization couldn't stand it, they prefer light work such as "shuffling cards or dice" or "removing the spirits of Frumenta from the gaze of rude men" if somebody else becomes responsible for the damage. Around the festive board, they are unequalled for their verbosity and especially for their aptness in tracing their ancestry. One will carry you away back to the times of William the Silent and bring you up to 18 so and so, to show how illustrious is his lineage and pedigree. His great, great grandfather's mother-in-law was the Marchioness So and So and his father was ex-Chief Justice Chastity of S. C. or some other southern state with a polygamous record.[2]

Washington became, in fact, the center of Negro "society" and retained this distinction until after the first World War. This was owing partly to the fact that until the mass migrations of Negroes to northern cities, Washington with around 90,000 Negroes had a larger Negro community than any city in the United States until 1920. The pre-eminence of Washington as the center of Negro "society" was due more especially to other factors. Because of its relatively large Negro professional class, including teachers in the segregated public school system, doctors, dentists, and lawyers, and large numbers of Negroes employed in the federal government, Negroes in the nation's capital had incomes far above those in other parts of the country. This enabled Washington's "colored society" to engage in forms of consumption and entertainment that established its pre-eminence among American Negroes. Moreover, the Negro "society" which developed in Washington was composed of the upper-class mulattoes who, in fleeing from persecution and discriminations in the South, brought to Washington the social distinctions and color snobbery that had been the basis of their ascendancy in the South.

The first World War, which initiated a period of increased social as well as physical mobility in the Negro population, set in motion social and economic forces that inaugurated a new stage in the evolution of Negro "society." First, family background and color snobbishness based upon white ancestry became less important for membership among the social elite. Although in Charleston, South Carolina, in Atlanta, Georgia, in New Orleans, and in other southern cities, Negro "society" might continue to boast of the white or mulatto ancestors, in New York, Chicago, and Detroit, those who were becoming "socially" prominent were beginning to ask, "What is his profession?" or "What is his income?" Even in Washington, where a light complexion had been so important in "society," these questions were being asked. "Blue veins" and "auburn hair and finely chiseled features" were beginning to be ridiculed as a basis of social prominence. A newspaper edited by a pure black Negro carried articles each week showing up the foibles of the mulattoes who constituted Negro "society."[3]

During a decade or so following the first World War, in both northern and southern cities education and occupation increasingly supplanted family background and a light complexion as a basis for admission to the social elite among Negroes. For example, in New York, Chicago, and Philadelphia, Negroes who had constituted Negro "society" because they were mulattoes and acted like "gentlemen" were pushed aside because they were engaged in personal services. The Negro doctors, dentists, lawyers, and businessmen, who could not boast of white ancestors or did not know their white ancestors, were becoming the leaders of Negro "society." Even if they did not act like "gentlemen," they were able to imitate white "society" in their standards of consumption and entertainment. In fact, they tended to ridicule the so-called "culture" and exclusiveness of the older Negro "society."

During this transition period in the development of Negro "society," the "socially" prominent among Negroes were developing the new social values and new orientation towards the American environment that have become characteristic of Negro "society" at the present time. Although among isolated enclaves in the Negro communities of both southern and northern cities there is an attempt to constitute a "social" elite after the manner of the older Negro "society," such Negroes are generally looked upon as curiosities. Family background has little significance in Negro "society" of the present day, although there is an unavowed color snobbishness which has ceased to have much importance. Education from the standpoint of fundamental culture has completely lost its significance. There is still a certain snobbishness in regard to one's occupation, but the most important thing about one's occupation is the amount of income which it brings. Therefore, at the present time, Negro "society" is constituted largely of professional and business men and women with large incomes that enable them to engage in conspicuous consumption. From time to time the incomes of these Negro professional men who are "socially" prominent are revealed to have been derived from traffic in narcotics and performing abortions, while it is difficult at times to determine whether "socially" prominent businessmen are engaged in legitimate or illegitimate business.[4]

## 2. The Gaudy Carnival

One may get some idea of the nature of "society" in the make-believe world of the black bourgeoisie from an article entitled "Society Rulers of 20 Cities," which was published in the May, 1949 issue of *Ebony*. The rulers of "society" included five wives of physicians, three wives of dentists, three women school teachers, two wives of morticians, a social worker, the owner of a newspaper, the wife of a lawyer, a banker's daughter, a concert pianist, and the wife of a college president. Of course, there are Negro women in these cities who would challenge the "social" ascendancy of these so-called leaders, since there is much competition to be known as a ruler of "society." In northern cities, especially, there are wives of politicians and businessmen who, because of their ability to engage in conspicuous consumption, would not accept these so-called leaders. Nevertheless, the rulers of "society" reported in *Ebony* are representative, on the whole, of the leaders in "society" among the black bourgeoisie both with respect to the source of income and the style of life of this element among the black bourgeoisie.

One of the rulers of colored society, a physician's wife who works every day, is celebrated for her three big parties each year. The ruler of society in a southern city has gained fame because she entertains Negroes who have a national reputation. Another has gained notoriety because she is a friend of Lena Horne and gave a cocktail party for the famous movie actress. A former social worker is reported to have won her position in "society" because certain white writers and white "playboys" have paid attention to her. Another gave lavish debutante parties for her daughters. A southern ruler of society seemingly won eminence because her husband gave her a Cadillac automobile and a mink coat. The eminence of one school teacher in society seems to stem from the fact that she gives expensive parties and drives a Mercury automobile. A physician and his wife who had been to Europe proved their "social" eminence by giving a "continental" dinner consisting of nine courses for fifty-six guests which required four hours and thirty-five minutes to consume. In one case the reader learns that a particular ruler of "society" is noted for receptions in her home, the walls and ceilings of which, including the bathroom, are covered with mirrors. Details are supplied concerning the other rulers of "society" who own Cadillacs, have elaborate recreation rooms, and supply unlimited food and liquor to their guests.

For that section of the black bourgeoisie which devotes itself to "society," life has become a succession of carnivals. In cities all over the country, Negro "society" has inaugurated Debutante Balls or Cotillions which provide an opportunity every year for the so-called rich Negroes to indulge in lavish expenditures and create a world of fantasy to satisfy their longing for recognition. Very often these "rich" Negroes mortgage their homes in order to maintain the fiction that they are able to indulge in these vast spectacles of make-believe. In Philadelphia the Debutante Ball known as the "Pink Cotillion" is reputed to excel all others in the country. At this Debutante Ball, noted for the money spent on decorations and the expensive gowns and jewels worn by the women, an award is made each year to some distinguished Negro. This award consists of a diamond cross of Malta. During the years 1949, 1950, and 1951, the diamond cross of Malta was presented successively to Marian

Anderson, Dr. Ralph Bunche, and Mrs. Mary McCleod Bethune.[5] The Debutante Balls are written up in the Negro press, with pictures, in order to show the splendor and wealth of those who participate in this world of make-believe.[6]

The Debutante Balls are only one manifestation of the carnival spirit of Negro "society" which never slackens, especially since the black bourgeoisie has been enjoying unusual prosperity during recent years. The weekly accounts in the Negro press of the activities of Negro "society" are invariably stories of unbridled extravagance. These stories include a catalogue of the jewelry, the gowns, and mink coats worn by the women, often accompanied by an estimate of the value of the clothes and jewelry, and the cost of the parties which they attend. One constantly reads of "chauffeured" Cadillac cars in which they ride to parties and of the cost of the homes in which they live. The carnival spirit of Negro "society" with its emphasis upon conspicuous consumption has permeated the Negro colleges, where the fraternities and sororities compete with each other to excel in the amount of money spent for flowers, decorations and entertainment. It was reported in the Negro press that during the Christmas holidays in 1952, nine Greek letter societies meeting in four cities spent $2,225,000.[7] Most of the persons attending the college fraternities and sororities were not, of course, college students, but as the article stated, top "social" and intellectual leaders. For these top "social" and intellectual leaders, the fraternities and sororities represented their most serious interest in life.

## 3. Playing Seriously

For a large section of the black bourgeoisie, their activities as members of "society" are their most serious or often their only serious preoccupation. Their preoccupation with "society" has its roots in the traditions of the Negro community in the United States. As we have seen above, in their position of house servants during slavery, Negroes acquired from their white masters notions of what constituted "social" life or "society." After emancipation they continued in the role of personal servants, and therefore saw the white man only in his home or when he was engaged in recreation. They never saw the white man at work in the shop or factory and when he engaged in the serious matter of business. As a consequence they devoted much time and much of their meager resources in attempting to carry on a form of "social" life similar to the whites'. For many Negroes, it appears that "social" life became identified with the condition of freedom. "Social" life among the masses of Negroes was a free and spontaneous expression of their desire to escape from the restraints of work and routine. But for those who set themselves apart as Negro "society," "social" life became a more formalized activity. Among the Negro elite as well as among the masses, "social" life acquired a significance that it did not have among white Americans.

The great significance which "social" life has for Negroes has been due to their exclusion from participation in American life.[8] The numerous "social" clubs and other forms of voluntary associations which have existed among them provided a form of participation that compensated for their rejection by the white community. At the same time these various "social" clubs have been a part of the struggle of Negroes for status within their segregated communities. The elite, who have set themselves apart as Negro "society" and have attempted to maintain an exclusive "social" life, have been extremely conscious of their inferior status in American life. For them "social" life has not only provided a form of participation; it has represented an effort to achieve identification with upper-class whites by imitating as far as possible the behavior of white "society."

The exclusion of middle-class Negroes from participation in the general life of the American community has affected their entire outlook on life. It has meant that whites did not take Negroes seriously; that whites did not regard the activities of Negroes as of any real consequence in American life. It has tended to encourage a spirit of irresponsibility or an attitude of "play" or make-believe among them. Consequently, Negroes have "played" at conducting their schools, at running their businesses, and at practicing their professions.[9] The spirit of play or make-believe has tended to distort or vitiate the ends of their most serious activities. For example, in a number of cities where Negro doctors have been excluded from joining the white professional association, they have set up "reading societies," supposedly to offset such exclusion. But, on the whole, these "reading societies" have turned out to be "social" clubs for drinking and playing poker. Playing, then, has become the one activity which the Negro may take seriously.

In fact, great importance is attached to "Negro society" in the Negro press because it is a serious preoccupation among the black bourgeoisie. One can get some notion of its importance from an editorial in the September, 1953, number of *Ebony* entitled "Is Negro Society Phony?" The editorial asserts that those who say that Negro "society" is a pretense are envious of those who have been accepted by "society." It goes on to show that members of American white "society" have achieved entrance in the same manner as the members of Negro "society." Then the editorial points out that people like Dr. Bunche, Louis Armstrong, Marian Anderson, Mary McCleod Bethune and Joe Louis have won their places in Negro "society" by achievement. The article concludes with the statement that brains rather than blood should be the basis for admission to Negro "society" and that if this is made the basis of acceptance, then Negro youth will seek recognition by Negro "society." It seemingly never occurred to the writer of the editorial that Negroes with brains would prefer not to seek escape in the world of make-believe of the black bourgeoisie.

The exaggerated importance which the black bourgeoisie attaches to "society" is revealed in the emphasis placed by the Negro press upon the "social" aspects of events concerning Negroes. When it was announced recently that a Negro businessman had been named a member of the American delegation to the United Nations, it was stated in a leading Negro publication that he was invading the "glittering international UN scene—the most exclusive and powerful *social* set in the world."[10] The news item added that the nominee had "already made plans to acquire new formal wear" and that he was preparing his wardrobe for his entrance into the United Nations. In fact, generally when white middle-class people have sought the co-operation of the black bourgeoisie in some serious community project, they have found it difficult unless it could be interpreted as a "social" event. For example, such liberal middle-class white groups as the League of Women Voters and League of Women Shoppers have constantly complained that they could not interest middle-class Negro women. On the other hand, let us take the following account of an interracial group of women who raised money for the fight against infantile paralysis. There appeared in the February 25, 1954, issue of *Jet,* under the section labeled "People Are Talking About," the statement that $1,500 was raised by a group of fifteen white and colored "society" women who wore over $500,000 worth of furs and gowns.

Anyone who achieves any distinction in any field may become a "socialite" in the Negro press. It is not simply that, as a Negro journalist stated, "anybody not in the criminal class can get a 'personal' or 'social' note in the Negro paper."[11] This suggests only a small-town attitude which may be found among any people. In making a "socialite" of a Negro, the Negro press is attributing to him or to her the highest conceivable status and recognition. For example, when a Negro anthropologist, who never attended "social" functions, gave a lecture in Chicago, the account in the Negro press referred to him as a "socialite." Consequently, one learns in the Negro press that wives of gamblers, policemen, waiters, college professors, doctors, lawyers, petty civil servants, and public school teachers are all "socialites"—often when their husbands are not so designated. It should be pointed out, however, that being called a "socialite" in the Negro press is generally regarded as a high compliment by the members of the black bourgeoisie, whatever may be their occupations.

As a consequence of the prestige of "society," many Negro professional men and women take more seriously their recreation than their professions. Once the writer heard a Negro doctor who was prominent "socially" say that he would rather lose a patient than have his favorite baseball team lose a game. This was an extreme expression of the relative value of professional work and recreation among the black bourgeoisie. At the same time, it is indicative of the value which many Negro professional men and women, including college professors, place upon sports. Except when they are talking within the narrow field of their professions, their conversations are generally limited to sports—baseball and football. They follow religiously the scores of the various teams and the achievements of all the players. For hours they listen to the radio accounts of sports and watch baseball and football games television. They become learned in the comments of sportswriters. Often they make long journeys in order to see their favorite teams—white or Negro—play baseball and football games. Although they may pretend to appreciate "cultural" things, this class as a whole has no real appreciation of art, literature, or music. One reads, for example, under what "People Are Talking About" in the September 2, 1954, issue of *Jet,* that a "wealthy" Negro doctor in Detroit is planning to install a "Hammond organ" on his "luxurious yacht." The decor of their homes reveals the most atrocious and childish tastes. Expensive editions of books are bought for decoration and left unread. The black bourgeoisie, especially the section which forms Negro "society," scarcely ever read books for recreation. Consequently, their conversation is trivial and exhibits a childish view of the world.

The prominent role of sports in the "serious playing" of Negro "society" stems partly from certain traditions in the Negro community. It reflects to some extent the traditions of the "gentleman" who engaged in no serious work. But in addition, preoccupation of Negro "society" with sports is related to its preoccupation with gambling, especially poker. This latter preoccupation is especially significant because it is related to the religious outlook of the black bourgeoisie, especially Negro "society."

## 4. From Church to Chance

The black bourgeoisie can not escape completely from the religious traditions of the Negro masses, since many of those who are achieving middle-class status have come from the masses. They are often haunted by the fears and beliefs which were instilled in them during their childhood. However, they are glad to escape from the prohibitions which the Baptists and Methodists placed upon dancing, card playing, and gambling. They want to escape from the concern of the Baptists and Methodists with sin and death and salvation. The middle-class Negro is like the "suburban agnostic" with whom Mary Kingsley compared the missionary-made African, who keeps the idea of the immortality of the soul and a future heaven but discards the unpleasant idea of hell.[12] The middle-class Negro will tell you that he believes in a Supreme Being, some vague entity who runs the universe, and the immortality of the soul, but he does not believe in hell because he thinks that man has his hell on earth. As a rule, the black bourgeoisie do not give themselves to reflection on these matters. They are regarded as impractical and unpleasant questions which should be left to a few "queer" Negroes, who should spend their time more profitably in making money. An outstanding educated Negro minister, who is a sort of a mystic, was generally regarded with amusement by the black bourgeoisie, and he sought a more congenial audience in an interracial church and as a visiting preacher in white colleges.

When the middle-class Negro abandons the traditional religion of his ancestors, he seldom adopts a new philosophical orientation in regard to existence and the world about him. Since he is as isolated intellectually as he is socially in the American environment, he knows nothing of humanistic philosophy and he rejects materialism because of his prejudices based upon ignorance. Negro intellectuals have nothing to offer him, since they have never developed a social philosophy, except perhaps a crude and unsophisticated opportunism. Therefore, as a rule, the middle-class Negro is the prey of all forms of spiritualism. He avoids the fantastic extravagances of Father Divine's cult, partly because lower-class Negroes are associated with it. He concedes, however, that Father Divine "does some good" because his followers are "honest and faithful domestic servants." Nevertheless, the black bourgeoisie are interested in "psychic" phenomena because, according to them, "scientists do not know everything." Therefore, the little reading in which they indulge is often concerned with "faith healing" and popular accounts of "psychic" phenomena. In some cities it has become a fad for members of Negro "society" to make a novena though they are not Catholics, and they have reported that this religious exercise has resulted in their securing a dress or mink coat which they have always desired.

Without the traditional religion of the Negro and a philosophy to give them an orientation towards life, the black bourgeoisie, especially the element among them known as Negro "society," have often become the worshippers of the God of Chance. This new faith or dependence upon chance finds its extreme expression in their preoccupation with gambling, including the "numbers" (the illegal lotteries in American cities), betting on horses, and more especially poker. At one time the black bourgeoisie regarded the "numbers" as a lower-class form of gambling and restricted themselves to betting on horses. Likewise, playing poker was formerly regarded by them as a pastime for the sporting element among Negroes. But with the emergence of the new Negro "society," playing the "numbers" has become respectable. This is not strange, since some members of "society" derive their incomes from the "numbers." Therefore, it is not unusual for Negro professional men and their wives to play the "numbers" daily. Even the wives of Negro college professors are sometimes "writers" or collectors of "numbers" for the "numbers racket."

But poker has become the most important form of recreation for members of "society" among the black bourgeoisie. In fact, poker is more than a form of recreation; it is the one absorbing interest of Negro "society." It is the chief subject of conversation. Negro "society" women talk over the telephone for hours on the last poker game. According to an article in *Ebony*, March, 1953, the bane of many "society" editors is that "social" affairs turn into poker games, though the latter "can be exciting" when the stakes involve "homes, lots, and automobiles." Even a chance encounter of members of Negro "society" will lead to a poker game. Moreover, poker has tended to level all social barriers among Negroes. At the richly furnished homes of Negro doctors, chauffeurs, waiters, gasoline station attendants gather with college professors to play poker. So important has poker become among the black bourgeoisie that the measure of a man has become the amount of stakes which he can place at a poker game.

In many cities of the United States, the black bourgeoisie usually spend their weekends in what might be called "poker marathons" or "poker orgies" which last sometimes from Friday night until Monday morning. Some poker players who still have old-fashioned religious ideas may leave the poker table long enough to go to church, because, as they say, they believe in God. But usually most of them, being refreshed with food, remain throughout the "marathon." Some college professors boast of leaving the poker table and going directly to lecture to their classes on Monday. Likewise, Negro surgeons have been heard to boast of leaving the poker table and going directly to perform an operation. Because of their devotion to poker, some middle-class Negroes form groups and journey periodically from city to city in order to engage in these gambling orgies. News of these orgies, with details emphasizing the high stakes played are the main topic of conversation among Negro "society." The importance of poker may be measured by the fact that some middle-class Negroes assert that poker is the one thing in life that prevents them from going crazy. Therefore, the role of poker as a "religious" force in the lives of the black bourgeoisie can not be discounted.

The activities of Negro "society" are an extreme expression of the world of make-believe. In the following chapter we shall look behind the masks of those who play a role in this spectacle and in the world of the black bourgeoisie generally.

# Chapter X

## Behind the Masks

SINCE THE BLACK BOURGEOISIE live largely in a world of make-believe, the masks which they wear to play their sorry roles conceal the feelings of inferiority and of insecurity and the frustrations that haunt their inner lives. Despite their attempt to escape from real identification with the masses of Negroes, they can not escape the mark of oppression any more than their less favored kinsmen. In attempting to escape identification with the black masses, they have developed a self-hatred that reveals itself in their deprecation of the physical and social characteristics of Negroes. Likewise, their feelings of inferiority and insecurity are revealed in their pathological struggle for status within the isolated Negro world and craving for recognition in the white world. Their escape into a world of make-believe with its sham "society" leaves them with a feeling of emptiness and futility which causes them to constantly seek an escape in new delusions.

## 1. The Mark of Oppression

There is an attempt on the part of the parents in middle-class families to shield their children against racial discrimination and the contempt of whites for colored people. Sometimes the parents go to fantastic extremes, such as prohibiting the use of the words "Negro" or "colored" in the presence of their children.[1] They sometimes try to prevent their children from knowing that they can not enter restaurants or other public places because they are Negroes, or even that the schools they attend are segregated schools for Negroes. Despite such efforts to insulate their children against a hostile white world, the children of the black bourgeoisie can not escape the mark of oppression. This is strikingly revealed in the statement of a seventeen-year-old middle-class Negro youth. When asked if he felt inferior in the presence of white people, he gave the following answer—which was somewhat unusual for its frankness but typical of the attitude of the black bourgeoisie:

> Off-hand, I'd say no, but actually knowing all these things that are thrown up to you about white people being superior—that they look more or less down upon all Negroes —that we have to look to them for everything we get—that they'd rather think of us as mice than men—I don't believe I or any other Negro can help but feel inferior. My father says that it isn't so—that we feel only inferior to those whom we feel are superior. But I don't believe we can feel otherwise. Around white people until I know them a while I feel definitely out of place. Once I played a ping-pong match with a white boy whose play I know wasn't as good as mine, and boys he managed to beat I beat with ease, but I just couldn't get it out of my mind that I way playing a white boy. Sort of an Indian sign on me, you know.[2]

The statement of this youth reveals how deep-seated is the feeling of inferiority, from which even the most favored elements among Negroes can not escape. However much some middle-class Negroes may seek to soothe their feeling of inferiority in an attitude which they often express in the adage, "it is better to reign in hell than serve in heaven," they are still conscious of their inferior status in American society. They may say, as did a bewildered middle-class youth, that they are proud of being a Negro or proud of being a member of the upper stratum in the Negro community and feel sorry for the Negro masses "stuck in the mud," but they often confess, as did this youth:

> However, knowing that there are difficulties that confront us all as Negroes, if I could be born again and had my choice I'd really want to be a white boy—I mean white or my same color, providing I could occupy the same racial and economic level I now enjoy. I am glad I am this color —I'm frequently taken for a foreigner. I wouldn't care to be lighter or darker and be a Negro. I am the darkest one

in the family due to my constant outdoor activities. I realize of course that there are places where I can't go despite my family or money just because I happen to be a Negro. With my present education, family background, and so forth, if I was only white I could go places in life. A white face holds supreme over a black one despite its economic and social status. Frankly, it leaves me bewildered.[3]

Not all middle-class Negroes consciously desire, as this youth, to be white in order to escape from their feelings of inferiority. In fact, the majority of middle-class Negroes would deny having the desire to be white, since this would be an admission of their feeling of inferiority. Within an intimate circle of friends some middle-class Negroes may admit that they desire to be white, but publicly they would deny any such wish. The black bourgeoisie constantly boast of their pride in their identification as Negroes. But when one studies the attitude of this class in regard to the physical traits or the social characteristics of Negroes, it becomes clear that the black bourgeoisie do not really wish to be identified with Negroes.

## 2. Insecurities and Frustrations

Since the black bourgeoisie can not escape identification with Negroes, they experience certain feelings of insecurity because of their feeling of inferiority. Their feeling of inferiority is revealed in their fear of competition with whites. There is first a fear of competition with whites for jobs. Notwithstanding the fact that middle-class Negroes are the most vociferous in demanding the right to compete on equal terms with whites, many of them still fear such competition. They prefer the security afforded by their monopoly of certain occupations within the segregated Negro community. For example, middle-class Negroes demand that the two Negro medical schools be reserved for Negro students and that a quota be set for white students, though Negro students are admitted to "white" medical schools. Since the Supreme Court of the United States has ruled against segregated public schools, many Negro teachers, even those who are well-prepared, fear that they can not compete with whites for teaching positions. Although this fear stems principally from a feeling of inferiority which is experienced generally by Negroes, it has other causes.

The majority of the black bourgeoisie fear competition with whites partly because such competition would mean that whites were taking them seriously, and consequently they would have to assume a more serious and responsible attitude towards their work. Middle-class Negroes, who are notorious for their inefficiency in the management of various Negro institutions, excuse their inefficiency on the grounds that Negroes are a "young race" and, therefore, will require time to attain the efficiency of the white man. The writer has heard a Negro college president, who has constantly demanded that Negroes have equality in American life, declare before white people in extenuation of the shortcomings of his own administration, that Negroes were a "child race" and that they had "to crawl before they could walk." Such declarations, while flattering to the whites, are revealing in that they manifest the black bourgeoisie's contempt for the Negro masses, while excusing its own deficiencies by attributing them to the latter. Yet it is clear that the black workers who must gain a living in a white man's mill or factory and in competition with white workers can not offer any such excuse for his inefficiency.

The fear of competition with whites is probably responsible for the black bourgeoisie's fear of competence and first-rate performance within its own ranks. When a Negro is competent and insists upon first-rate work it appears to this class that he is trying to be a white man, or that he is insisting that Negroes measure up to white standards. This is especially true where the approval of whites is taken as a mark of competence and first-rate performance. In such cases the black bourgeoisie reveal their ambivalent attitudes toward the white world. They slavishly accept the estimate which almost any white man places upon a Negro or his work, but at the same time they fear and reject white standards. For example, when a group of Negro doctors were being shown the modern equipment and techniques of a white clinic, one of them remarked to a Negro professor in a medical school, "This is the white man's medicine. I never bother with it and still I make $30,000 a year." Negroes who adopt the standards of the white world create among the black bourgeoisie a feeling of insecurity and often become the object of both the envy and hatred of this class.

Among the women of the black bourgeoisie there is an intense fear of the competition of white women for Negro men. They often attempt to rationalize their fear by saying that the Negro man always occupies an inferior position in relation to the white woman or that he marries much below his "social" status. They come nearer to the source of their fear when they confess that there are not many eligible Negro men and that these few should marry Negro women. That such rationalizations conceal deep-seated feelings of insecurity is revealed by the fact that generally they have no objection to the marriage of white men to Negro women, especially if the white man is reputed to be wealthy. In fact, they take pride in the fact and attribute these marriages to the "peculiar" charms of Negro women. In fact, the middle-class Negro woman's fear of the competition of white women is based often upon the fact that she senses her own inadequacies and shortcomings. Her position in Negro "society" and in the larger Negro community is often due to some adventitious factor, such as a light complexion or a meager education, which has pushed her to the top of the social pyramid. The middle-class white woman not only has a white skin and straight hair, but she is generally more sophisticated and interesting because she has read more widely and has a larger view of the world. The middle-class Negro woman may make fun of the "plainness" of her white competitor and the latter's lack of "wealth" and interest in "society"; nevertheless she still feels insecure when white women appear as even potential competitors.

Both men and women among the black bourgeoisie have a feeling of insecurity because of their constant fear of the loss of status. Since they have no status in the larger American society, the intense struggle for status among middle-class Negroes is, as we have seen, an attempt to compensate for the contempt and low esteem of the whites. Great value is, therefore, placed upon all kinds of status symbols. Academic degrees, both real and honorary, are sought in order to secure status. Usually the symbols are of a material nature implying wealth and conspicuous consumption. Sometimes Negro doctors do not attend what are supposedly scientific meetings because they do not have a Cadillac or some other expensive automobile. School teachers wear mink coats and maintain homes beyond their income for fear that they may lose status. The extravagance in "social" life generally is due to an effort not to lose status. But in attempting to overcome their fear of loss of status they are often beset by new feelings of insecurity. In spite of their pretended wealth, they are aware that their incomes are insignificant and that they must struggle to maintain their mortgaged homes and the show of "wealth" in lavish "social" affairs. Moreover, they are beset by a feeling of insecurity because of their struggles to maintain a show of wealth through illegal means. From time to time "wealthy" Negro doctors are arrested for selling narcotics and performing abortions. The life of many a "wealthy" Negro doctor is shortened by the struggle to provide diamonds, minks, and an expensive home for his wife.

There is much frustration among the black bourgeoisie despite their privileged position within the segregated Negro world. Their "wealth" and "social" position can not erase the fact that they are generally segregated and rejected by the white world. Their incomes and occupations may enable them to escape the cruder manifestations of racial prejudice, but they can not insulate themselves against the more subtle forms of racial discrimination. These discriminations cause frustrations in Negro men because they are not allowed to play the "masculine role" as defined by American culture. They can not assert themselves or exercise power as white men do. When they protest against racial discrimination there is always the threat that they will be punished by the white world. In spite of the movement toward the wider integration of the Negro into the general stream of American life, middle-class Negroes are still threatened with the loss of positions and earning power if they insist upon their rights.[4] After the Supreme Court of the United States ruled that segregation in public education was illegal, Negro teachers in some parts of the South were dismissed because they would not sign statements supporting racial segregation in education.

As one of the results of not being able to play the "masculine role," middle-class Negro males have tended to cultivate their "personalities"[5] which enable them to exercise considerable influence among whites and achieve distinction in the Negro world. Among Negroes they have been noted for their glamour.[6] In this respect they resemble women who use their "personalities" to compensate for their inferior status in relation to men. This fact would seem to support the observation of an American sociologist that the Negro was "the lady among the races," if he had restricted his observation to middle-class males among American Negroes.[7]

In the South the middle-class Negro male is not only prevented from playing a masculine role, but generally he must let Negro women assume leadership in any show of militancy. This reacts upon his status in the home where the tradition of female dominance, which is widely established among Negroes, has tended to assign a subordinate role to the male. In fact, in middle-class families, especially if the husband has risen in social status through his own efforts and married a member of an "old" family or a "society" woman, the husband is likely to play a pitiful role. The greatest compliment that can be paid such a husband is that he "worships his wife," which means that he is her slave and supports all her extravagances and vanities. But, of course, many husbands in such positions escape from their frustrations by having extra-marital sex relations. Yet the conservative and conventional middle-class husband presents a pathetic picture. He often sits at home alone, impotent physically and socially, and complains that his wife has gone crazy about poker and "society" and constantly demands money for gambling and expenditures which he can not afford. Sometimes he enjoys the sympathy of a son or daughter who has not become a "socialite." Such children often say that they had a happy family life until "mamma took to poker."

Preoccupation with poker on the part of the middle-class woman is often a attempt to escape from a frustrated life.

Her frustration may be bound up with her unsatisfactory sexual life. She may be married to a "glamorous" male who neglects her for other women. For among the black bourgeoisie, the glamour of the male is often associated with his sexual activities. The frustration of many Negro women has a sexual origin.[8] Even those who have sought an escape from frustration in sexual promiscuity may, because of satiety or deep psychological reasons, become obsessed with poker in order to escape from their frustrations. One "society" woman, in justification of her obsession with poker remarked that it had taken the place of her former preoccupation with sex. Another said that to win at poker was similar to a sexual orgasm.

The frustration of the majority of the women among the black bourgeoisie is probably due to the idle or ineffectual lives which they lead. Those who do not work devote their time to the frivolities of Negro "society." When they devote their time to "charity" or worth-while causes, it is generally a form of play or striving for "social" recognition. They are constantly forming clubs which ostensibly have a serious purpose, but in reality are formed in order to consolidate their position in "society" or to provide additional occasions for playing poker. The idle, overfed women among the black bourgeoisie are generally, to use their language, "dripping with diamonds." They are forever dieting and reducing only to put on more weight (which is usually the result of the food that they consume at their club meetings). Even the women among the black bourgeoisie who work exhibit the same frustrations. Generally, they have no real interest in their work and only engage in it in order to be able to provide the conspicuous consumption demanded by "society." As we have indicated, the women as well as the men among the black bourgeoisie read very little and have no interest in music, art or the theater. They are constantly restless and do not know how to relax. They are generally dull people and only become animated when "social" matters are discussed, especially poker games. They are afraid to be alone and constantly seek to be surrounded by their friends, who enable them to escape from their boredom.

The frustrated lives of the black bourgeoisie are reflected in the attitudes of parents towards their children. Middle-class Negro families as a whole have few children, while among the families that constitute Negro "society" there are many childless couples.[9] One finds today, as an American observed over forty years ago, that "where the children are few, they are usually spoiled" in middle-class Negro families.[10] There is often not only a deep devotion to their one or two children, but a subservience to them. It is not uncommon for the only son to be called and treated as the "boss" in the family. Parents cater to the transient wishes of their children and often rationalize their behavior towards them on the grounds that children should not be "inhibited." They spend large sums of money on their children for toys and especially for clothes. They provide their children with automobiles when they go to college. All of this is done in order that the children may maintain the status of the parents and be eligible to enter the "social" set in Negro colleges. When they send their children to northern "white" colleges they often spend more time in preparing them for what they imagine will be their "social" life than in preparing them for the academic requirements of these institutions.

In their fierce devotion to their children, which generally results in spoiling them, middle-class Negro parents are seemingly striving at times to establish a human relationship that will compensate for their own frustrations in the realm of human relationships. Devotion to their children often becomes the one human tie that is sincere and free from the competition and artificiality of the make-believe world in which they live. Sometimes they may project upon their children their own frustrated professional ambitions. But usually, even when they send their children to northern "white" universities as a part of their "social" striving within the Negro community, they seem to hope that their children will have an acceptance in the white world which has been denied them.

## 3. Self-Hatred and Guilt Feelings

One of the chief frustrations of the middle-class Negro is

that he can not escape identification with the Negro race and
consequently is subject to the contempt of whites.* Despite
his "wealth" in which he has placed so much faith as a sol-
vent of racial discrimination, he is still subject to daily insults
and is excluded from participation in white American society. Middle-class Negroes do not express their resentment
against discrimination and insults in violent outbreaks, as
lower-class Negroes often do. They constantly repress their
hostility toward whites and seek to soothe their hurt self-
esteem in all kinds of rationalizations. They may boast of
their wealth and culture as compared with the condition of
the poor whites. Most often they will resort to any kind of
subterfuge in order to avoid contact with whites. For example, in the South they often pay their bills by mail rather
than risk unpleasant contacts with representatives of white
firms.[11] The daily repression of resentment and the constant
resort to means of avoiding contacts with whites do not
relieve them of their hostility toward whites. Even middle-
class Negroes who gain a reputation for exhibiting "objectivity" and a "statesmanlike" attitude on racial discrimination harbor deep-seated hostilities toward whites. A Negro
college president who has been considered such an inter-

---

* A Middle-class mulatto woman, a former school teacher, who
was fearful of the impact of this book on European readers and
southern detractors of "The Race," concluded her review of the
original French edition with these words:

"Isn't it about time our sociologists and specialists on the
'race problem' in America, began to discuss and consider middle
class Negroes as middle class Americans, or better, *all* U.S.
Negroes as *Americans* with three hundred unbroken years of
American tradition, way of life, cultural and spiritual contacts
behind them—influences which have moulded them as they
have moulded all others who are considered, even when not
treated completely so, as members of the American community?
Isn't it time to stop thinking of and talking about Negroes as a
separate and distinct entity in the general scheme of things?
And above all, isn't it time to realize that the melting pot has
melted truly and fused together all the myriad (albeit con-
flicting) racial, cultural, educational, spiritual and social elements which have combined in such peculiar fashion to produce
the American Negro of our time?" *Journal of Negro Education,*
Vol. XXV, p. 141.

racial "statesman" once confessed to the writer that some day he was going to "break loose" and tell white people what he really thought. However, it is unlikely that a middle-class Negro of his standing will ever "break loose." Middle-class Negroes generally express their aggressions against whites by other means, such as deceiving whites and utilizing them for their own advantage.

Because middle-class Negroes are unable to indulge in aggressions against whites as such, they will sometimes make other minority groups the object of their hostilities. For example, they may show hostility against Italians, who are also subject to discrimination. But more often middle-class Negroes, especially those who are engaged in a mad scramble to accumulate money, will direct their hostilities against Jews. They are constantly expressing their anti-semitism within Negro circles, while pretending publicly to be free from prejudice. They blame the Jew for the poverty of Negroes and for their own failures and inefficiencies in their business undertakings. In expressing their hostility towards Jews, they are attempting at the same time to identify with the white American majority.

The repressed hostilities of middle-class Negroes to whites are not only directed towards other minority groups but inward toward themselves. This results in self-hatred, which may appear from their behavior to be directed towards the Negro masses but which in reality is directed against themselves.[12] While pretending to be proud of being a Negro, they ridicule Negroid physical characteristics and seek to modify or efface them as much as possible. Within their own groups they constantly proclaim that "niggers" make them sick. The very use of the term "nigger," which they claim to resent, indicates that they want to disassociate themselves from the Negro masses. They talk condescendingly of Africans and of African culture, often even objecting to African sculpture in their homes. They are insulted if they are identified with Africans. They refuse to join organizations that are interested in Africa. If they are of mixed ancestry, they may boast of the fact that they have Indian ancestry. When making compliments concerning the beauty of Negroes of mixed ancestry, they generally say, for example, "She is beautiful; she looks like an Indian." On the other hand, if a black woman has European features, they will remark condescendingly, "Although she is black, you must admit that she is good looking." Some middle-class Negroes of mixed ancestry like to wear Hindu costumes—while they laugh at the idea of wearing an African costume. When middle-class Negroes travel, they studiously avoid association with other Negroes, especially if they themselves have received the slightest recognition by whites. Even when they can not "pass" for white they fear that they will lose this recognition if they are identified as Negroes. Therefore, nothing pleases them more than to be mistaken for a Puerto Rican, Philippino, Egyptian or Arab or any ethnic group other than Negro.

The self-hatred of middle-class Negroes is often revealed in the keen competition which exists among them for status and recognition. This keen competition is the result of the frustrations which they experience in attempting to obtain acceptance and recognition by whites. Middle-class Negroes are constantly criticizing and belittling Negroes who achieve some recognition or who acquire a status above them. They prefer to submit to the authority of whites than to be subordinate to other Negroes. For example, Negro scholars generally refuse to seek the advice and criticism of competent Negro scholars and prefer to turn to white scholars for such co-operation. In fact, it is difficult for middle-class Negroes to co-operate in any field of endeavor. This failure in social relations is, as indicated in an important study, because "in every Negro he encounters his own self-contempt."[13] It is as if he said, "You are only a Negro like myself; so why should you be in a position above me?"

This self-hatred often results in guilt feelings on the part of the Negro who succeeds in elevating himself above his fellows.[14] He feels unconsciously that in rising above other Negroes he is committing an act of aggression which will result in hatred and revenge on their part. The act of aggression may be imagined, but very often it is real. This is the case when middle-class Negroes oppose the economic and social welfare of Negroes because of their own interests. In some American cities, it has been the black bourgeoisie and not the whites who have opposed the building of low-cost public housing for Negro workers. In one city two wealthy Negro doctors, who have successfully opposed public housing projects for Negro workers, own some of the worst slums in the United States. While their wives, who wear mink coats, "drip with diamonds" and are written up in the "society" columns of Negro newspapers, ride in Cadillacs, their Negro tenants sleep on the dirt floors of hovels unfit for human habitation. The guilt feelings of the middle-class Negro are not always unconscious. For example, take the case of the Negro leader who proclaimed over the radio in a national broadcast that the Negro did not want social equity. He was conscious of his guilt feelings and his self-hatred in playing such a role, for he sent word privately to the writer that he never hated so much to do anything in his life, but that it was necessary because of his position as head of a state college which was under white supervision. The self-hatred of the middle-class Negro arises, then, not only from the fact that he does not want to be a Negro but also because of his sorry role in American society.

## 4. Escape into Delusions

The black bourgeoisie, as we have seen, has created a world of make-believe to shield itself from the harsh economic and social realities of American life. This world of make-believe is created out of the myth of Negro business, the reports of the Negro press on the achievements and wealth of Negroes, the recognition accorded them by whites, and the fabulous life of Negro "society." Some of the middle-class Negro intellectuals are not deceived by the world of make-believe. They will have nothing to do with Negro "society" and refuse to waste their time in frivolities. They take their work seriously and live in relative obscurity so far as the Negro world is concerned. Others seek an escape from their frustrations by developing, for example, a serious interest in Negro music—which the respectable black bourgeoisie often pretend to despise. In this way these intellectuals achieve some identification with the Negro masses and with the traditions of Negro life. But many more middle-class Negroes, who are satisfied to live in the world of make-believe but must find a solution to the real economic and social problems which they face, seek an escape in delusions.

They seek an escape in delusions involving wealth. This is facilitated by the fact that they have had little experience with the real meaning of wealth and that they lack a tradition of saving and accumulation. Wealth to them means spending money without any reference to its source. Hence, their behavior generally reflects the worst qualities of the gentleman and peasant from whom their only vital traditions spring. Therefore, their small accumulations of capital and the income which they receive from professional services within the Negro community make them appear wealthy in comparison with the low economic status of the majority of Negroes. The delusion of wealth is supported by the myth of Negro business. Moreover, the attraction of the delusion of wealth is enhanced by the belief that wealth will gain them acceptance in American life. In seeking an escape in the delusion of wealth, middle-class Negroes make a fetish of material things or physical possessions. They are constantly buying things—houses, automobiles, furniture and all sorts of gadgets, not to mention clothes. Many of the furnishings and gadgets which they acquire are never used; nevertheless they continue to accumulate things. The homes of many middle-class Negroes have the appearance of museums for the exhibition of American manufactures and spurious art objects. The objects which they are constantly buying are always on display. Negro school teachers who devote their lives to "society" like to display twenty to thirty pairs of shoes, the majority of which they never wear. Negro professional men proudly speak of the two automobiles which they have acquired when they need only one. The acquisition of objects which are not used or needed seems to be an attempt to fill some void in their lives.

The delusion of power also appears to provide an escape for middle-class Negroes from the world of reality which pierces through the world of make-believe of the black bourgeoisie. The positions of power which they occupy in the Negro world often enable them to act autocratically towards other Negroes, especially when they have the support of the white community. In such cases the delusion of power may provide an escape from their frustrations. It is generally, however, when middle-class Negroes hold positions enabling them to participate in the white community that they seek in the delusion of power an escape from their frustrations. Although their position may be only a "token" of the integration of the Negro into American life, they will speak and act as if they were a part of the power structure of American society. Negro advisers who are called into counsel by whites to give advice about Negroes are especially likely to find an escape from their feelings of inferiority in the delusion of power. Negro social workers, who are dependent upon white philanthropy, have often gained the reputation, with the support of the Negro press, of being powerful persons in American communities.

However, the majority of the black bourgeoisie who seek an escape from their frustrations in delusions seemingly have not been able to find it in the delusion of wealth or power. They have found it in magic or chance, and in sex and alcohol. Excessive drinking and sex seem to provide a means for narcotizing the middle-class Negro against a frustrating existence. A "social" function is hardly ever considered a success unless a goodly number of the participants "pass out." But gambling, especially poker, which has become an obsession among many middle-class Negroes, offers the chief escape into delusion. Among the black bourgeoisie it is not simply a device for winning money. It appears to be a magical device for enhancing their self-esteem through overcoming fate.[15] Although it often involves a waste of money which many middle-class Negroes can not afford, it has an irresistible attraction which they often confess they can not overcome.

Despite the tinsel, glitter and gaiety of the world of make-believe in which middle-class Negroes take refuge, they are still beset by feelings of insecurity, frustration and guilt. As a consequence, the free and easy life which they appear to lead is a mask for their unhappy existence.

# Conclusion

WHEN VIEWED IN the broad perspective of the changes which are occurring in the western world, this study of the black bourgeoisie reveals in an acute form many of the characteristics of modern bourgeois society, especially in the United States. Hence it was difficult to resist the temptation to compare the black bourgeoisie with the same class among white Americans. However, it was not the purpose of this study to isolate and analyze the common characteristics of this class in the modern world. Our task was less ambitious and therefore more restricted. Our purpose was to treat the black bourgeoisie as a case study of a middle-class group which had emerged during the changing adjustment of a racial minority to modern industrial society. From this standpoint our study may have a broader significance than the group which we have studied. It may have some relevance for the study of the emergence of a middle class in colonial societies, especially in African societies at present undergoing rapid changes. The characteristics of this class in the various societies will have to be studied in each case in relation to its history and the economic and social forces which are responsible for its development.

The black bourgeoisie in the United States is an essentially American phenomenon. Its emergence and its rise to importance within the Negro community are closely tied up with economic and social changes in the American community. Its behavior as well as its mentality is a reflection of American modes of behavior and American values. What may appear as distortions of American patterns of behavior and thought are due to the fact that the Negro lives on the margin of American society. The very existence of a separate Negro community with its own institutions within the heart of the American society is indicative of its quasi-pathological character, especially since the persistence of this separate community has been due to racial discrimination and oppression.

As the result of this fact, the black bourgeoisie is unique in a number of respects: First, it lacks a basis in the American economic system. Among colonial peoples and among other racial minorities, the bourgeoisie usually comes into existence as the result of its role in the economic organization of these societies. But the black bourgeoisie in the United States has subsisted off the crumbs of philanthropy, the salaries of public servants, and what could be squeezed from the meager earnings of Negro workers. Hence "Negro business," which has no significance in the American economy, has become a social myth embodying the aspirations of this class. Then, because of the position of the Negro in American life, it has been impossible for the black bourgeoisie to play the traditional role of this class among minorities. The attempt on the part of the Communist Party to assign to the black bourgeoisie the traditional role of this class, in what the Party defined as the struggle of the "Negro people" for "national liberation," only tended to emphasize the unreality of the position of the black bourgeoisie. Moreover, the black bourgeoisie have shown no interest in the "liberation" of Negroes except as it affected their own status or acceptance by the white community. They viewed with scorn the Garvey Movement with its nationalistics aims. They showed practically no interest in the Negro Renaissance. They wanted to forget the Negro's past, and they have attempted to conform to the behavior and values of the white community in the most minute details. Therefore they have often become, as has been observed, "exaggerated" Americans.

Because of its struggle to gain acceptance by whites, the black bourgeoisie has failed to play the role of a responsible elite in the Negro community. Many individuals among the first generation of educated Negroes, who were the products of missionary education, had a sense of responsibility toward the Negro masses and identified themselves with the struggles of the masses to overcome the handicaps of ignorance and poverty. Their influence over the masses was limited, to be sure—not, however, because of any lack of devotion on their part, but because of the control exercised by the white community. Nevertheless, they occupied a dignified position within the Negro community and were respected. As teachers of Negroes, they generally exhibited the same sincere interest in education and genuine culture as their missionary teachers. Therefore they did not regard teaching merely as a source of income. On the other hand, today many Negro teachers refuse identification with the Negro masses and look upon teaching primarily as a source of income. In many cases they have nothing but contempt for their Negro pupils. Moreover, they have no real interest in education and genuine culture and spend their leisure in frivolities and in activities designed to win a place in Negro "society."

When the opportunity has been present, the black bourgeoisie has exploited the Negro masses as ruthlessly as have whites. As the intellectual leaders in the Negro community, they have never dared think beyond a narrow, opportunistic philosophy that provided a rationalization for their own advantages. Although the black bourgeoisie exercise considerable influence on the values of Negroes, they do not occupy a dignified position in the Negro community. The masses regard the black bourgeoisie as simply those who have been "lucky in getting money" which enables them to engage in conspicuous consumption. When this class pretends to represent the best manners or morals of the Negro, the masses regard such claims as hypocrisy.

The single factor that has dominated the mental outlook of the black bourgeoisie has been its obsession with the struggle for status. The struggle for status has expressed itself mainly in the emphasis upon "social" life or "society." The concern of the Negro for "social" life and "society" has been partly responsible for the failure of educated Negroes to make important contributions within the fields of science or art. Educated Negroes have been constantly subjected to the pressures of the black bourgeoisie to conform to its values. Because of this pressure some gifted Negroes have abandoned altogether their artistic and scientific aspirations, while others have chosen to play the role of phony intellectuals and cater to the ignorance and vanities of the black bourgeoisie in order to secure "social" acceptance. Since middle-class Negroes have never been permitted to play a serious role in American life, "social" life has offered an area of competition in which the serious affairs of life were not involved. Middle-class Negroes who have made real contributions in science and art have had to escape from the influence of the "social" life of the black bourgeoisie. In fact, the spirit of play or lack of serious effort has permeated every aspect of the life of the Negro community. It has, therefore, tended to encourage immaturity and childishness on the part of middle-class Negroes, whose lives are generally devoted to trivialities.

The emphasis upon "social" life or "society" is one of the main props of the world of make-believe into which the black bourgeoisie has sought an escape from its inferiority and frustrations in American society. This world of make-believe, to be sure, is a reflection of the values of American society, but it lacks the economic basis that would give it roots in the world of reality. In escaping into a world of make-believe, middle-class Negroes have rejected both identification with the Negro and his traditional culture. Through delusions of wealth and power they have sought identification with the white America which continues to reject them. But these delusions leave them frustrated because they are unable to escape from the emptiness and futility of their existence. Gertrude Stein would have been nearer the truth if she had said of the black bourgeoisie what she said of Negroes in general, that they "were not suffering from persecution, they were suffering from nothingness," not because, as she explained, the African has "a very ancient but a very narrow culture."[1] The black bourgeoisie suffers from "nothingess" because when Negroes attain middle-class status, their lives generally lose both content and significance.

# Notes

## Introduction

1. According to the United States Census for 1960, the Negro population numbered 18,871,831. This figure does not include, of course, an unknown number of Negroes who have "passed" into the white race, or their offspring and descendants who have no knowledge of their Negro ancestry.

2. J. H. Parry, *Europe and a Wider World 1415-1715* (London: Hutchinson, 1949).

3. Eric Williams, *Capitalism and Slavery* (Chapel Hill: University of North Carolina Press, 1944), *passim.*

4. E. Franklin Frazier, *The Negro in the United States* (New York: Macmillan, 1949), Chapter II, "Evolution of the Slave System."

5. Frazier, *op. cit.,* Chapter III, "The Plantation as a Social Institution."

6. See Frazier, *op. cit.,* Chapter I. The position stated here has been challenged by Melville J. Herskovits, *The Myth of the Negro's Past* (New York: Harper, 1942). According to Herskovits, who has made a systematic and comprehensive study of African cultural survivals in the New World, many of the social characteristics of Negroes in the United States are attributable to African survivals. Nevertheless, Herskovits admits that there are fewer of these survivals, that they have become more attenuated, and that they are less easily recognized in the United States than in Brazil and the West Indies.

7. John H. Russell, *The Free Negro in Virginia: 1619-1865* (Baltimore: Johns Hopkins University Press, 1913), *passim.* On the free Negroes in the South before the Civil War, the following works may be consulted: Carter G. Woodson, *Free Negro Heads of Families in the United States in 1830* (Washington, D. C.: The Association for the Study of Negro Life and History, 1925); John Hope Franklin, *The Free Negro in North Carolina* (Chapel Hill: University of North Carolina Press, 1943); Luther P. Jackson, *Free Negro Labor and Property Holding in Virginia, 1830-1860* (New York: Appleton-Century-Crofts, 1942); Edward R. Turner, *The Negro in Pennsylvania* (Washington, D. C.: American Historical Association, 1911); James M. Wright, *The Free Negro in*

*Maryland, 1634-1860* (New York: Columbia University Press, 1921); Frazier, *op. cit.*, Chapter IV, "The Free Negro."

8. See Russell, *op. cit.*, and Wright, *op. cit.*

9. E. Horace Fitchett, "The Traditions of the Free Negroes in Charleston, South Carolina," *Journal of Negro History*, XXV, pp. 139-152.

10. Louis M. Hacker, *The Triumph of American Capitalism* (New York: Simon and Schuster, 1940).

11. John Hope Franklin, "Reconstruction," in Richard Leopold and Arthur Link (eds.) *Problems in American History* (New York: Prentice-Hall, 1952). See also W. E. Burghardt DuBois, *Black Reconstruction* (New York: Harcourt, Brace, 1935), and Paul Lewison, *Race, Class and Party* (New York: Oxford University Press, 1932).

12. Frazier, *op. cit.*, pp. 155-164.

13. W. E. Burghardt DuBois, "The Negro in the Black Belt: Some Social Sketches," *Bulletin of the [U.S.] Department of Labor*, No. 22, May, 1899. See also the sixteen monographs in the *Atlanta University Studies*, edited by W. E. B. DuBois, on the various aspects of the Negro life.

14. The Chicago Commission on Race Relations, *The Negro in Chicago* (Chicago: University of Chicago Press, 1922). See also, for later developments, St. Clair Drake and Horace R. Cayton, *Black Metropolis* (New York: Harcourt, Brace, 1945).

15. T. G. Standing, "Nationalism in Negro Leadership," *American Journal of Sociology*, XI, pp. 180-92. See also W. E. B. DuBois, "Marcus Garvey," *The Crisis*, December 1920 and January 1921, and E. Franklin Frazier, "Garvey: A Mass Leader," *The Nation*, August 18, 1926.

16. See Wilson Record, *The Negro and the Communist Party* (Chapel Hill: University of North Carolina Press, 1951), Chapter III.

17. See Herbert R. Northrop, *Organized Labor and the Negro* (New York: Harper, 1949); Horace R. Cayton and George R. Mitchell, *Black Workers and the New Unions* (Chapel Hill: University of North Carolina Press, 1939).

## Chapter I

## The Roots of the Black Bourgeoisie

1. See Abram L. Harris, *The Negro as Capitalist* (Philadelphia: American Academy of Political and Social Science, 1936), pp.

4-24, on the efforts of Negroes who were free before the Civil War to acquire wealth.

2. See *Documentary History of American Industrial Society— Plantation and Frontier Documents, 1649-1863* (Cleveland: Clark, 1909), I, "Introduction" by Ulrich B. Phillips, pp. 88-89.

3. Luther P. Jackson, *Free Negro Labor and Property Holding in Virginia, 1830-1860*, pp. 109-110.

4. John Hope Franklin, *The Free Negro in North Carolina*, pp. 158-59.

5. From unpublished manuscript of Charles Gayarre quoted in Grace King, *New Orleans: The Place and the People* (New York: Macmillan, 1928), pp. 344-46.

6. Carter G. Woodson, *Free Negro Heads of Families in the United States in 1830* (Washington, D. C.: Association for the Study of Negro Life and History, Inc., 1925), p. xxxv.

7. Harris, *op. cit.*, pp. 5-6.

8. *Ibid.*, p. 6.

9. Woodson, *op. cit.*

10. Harris, *op. cit.*, p. 710.

11. List of the taxpayers of the city of Charleston for 1860, pp. 315-34.

12. Harris, *op. cit.*, p. 8.

13. See Carter G. Woodson, *op. cit.*

14. Charles H. Wesley, *Negro Labor in the United States, 1850-1925* (New York: Vanguard, 1927); see Chapter II for occupations of free Negroes in Charleston, New York City, New Orleans, Boston, St. Louis, and Philadelphia.

15. George E. Haynes, *The Negro at Work in New York City* (New York: Columbia University Press, 1912), pp. 96-97.

16. Woodson, *op. cit.*, pp. xxxvii-xxxix.

17. Jackson, *op. cit.*, p. 76.

18. Harris, *op. cit.*, p. 9.

19. Harris, *op. cit.*, p. 3. See also Martin A. Delany, *Condition, Elevation, Emigration and Destiny of the Colored People of the United States* (Philadelphia: The Author, 1852), pp. 42-45.

20. See Werner Sombart, *The Quintessence of Capitalism* (London: Unwin, 1915), Chapter XI, "The Bourgeois—Old Style."

21. See Walter L. Fleming, *The Freedmen's Savings Bank* (Chapel Hill: University of North Carolina Press, 1927), pp. 19-27.

22. *Ibid.*, p. 30.

23. *Ibid.*, pp. 38-39.

24. See Abram L. Harris, *The Negro as Capitalist*, Chapter

II, "The Legacy of the Freedmen's Bank." This book is a definitive study of Negro banking from its beginning through 1932. Moreover, all of the conclusions of this study are valid for the period subsequent to 1932.

25. Frederick Douglass, *Life and Times of Frederick Douglass* (Chicago: J. B. Goodman and Company, 1882), pp. 410-11.

26. Fleming, *op. cit.*, pp. 129-30.

27. *Ibid.*, pp. 44-48.

28. Douglass, *op. cit.*, pp. 409-10.

29. Harris, *op. cit.*, p. 60.

30. *Ibid.*, p. 165.

31. *Ibid.*, p. 46.

32. *Ibid.*, p. 61.

33. Frazier, *op. cit.*, pp. 371 ff.

34. Harris, *op cit.*, p. 63.

35. Quoted in Harris, *ibid.*, p. 63.

36. *Ibid.*, p. 73. In the case of the numerous failures of Negro banks, there has been much dishonesty involving, for example, the use of the resources to promote enterprises for the officials of the banks. At the same time, the officials of Negro banks have often invested too much of the resources of the banks in unproductive buildings, furniture and fixtures, which have constituted as much as 25 per cent of the resources of the banks.

## Chapter II

## The Economic Basis of Middle-Class Status

1. See U. S. Department of Commerce, Bureau of the Census, *Negro Population, 1790-1915* (Washington: Government Printing Office, 1918), *passim*.

2. U. S. Department of Commerce, Bureau of the Census, *Negroes in the United States, 1920-1932* (Washington: Government Printing Office, 1935), Chapter XIV, "Occupations."

3. Frank Alexander Ross, "Urbanization and the Negro," *Publication of the American Sociological Society*, XXVI, pp. 115-28. See also Louis Venable Kennedy, *The Negro Peasant Turns Cityward* (New York: Columbia University Press, 1930).

4. See E. Franklin Frazier, "Occupational Classes Among Negroes in Cities," *American Journal of Sociology*, XXXV, pp. 718-38.

5. E. Franklin Frazier, *The Negro in the United States*, pp. 229 ff.

6. The southern cities were Atlanta, Birmingham, Memphis, and

New Orleans; the border cities, Baltimore, St. Louis, and Washington, D. C.; the northern cities, Chicago, Detroit, New York, and Philadelphia.

7. See John Hope, II, "The Employment of Negroes in the United States by Major Occupations and Industry," *Journal of Negro Education*, XXII, pp. 307-21.

8. *Ibid.*, p. 309.

9. *Ibid.*, note 8, p. 310.

10. See George S. Mitchell, "Money Income of Negroes in the United States," *Journal of Negro Education*, XXII, pp. 333-42.

11. In order to secure an estimate of the incomes of the black bourgeoisie, we have taken the same percentage of incomes in the top income brackets as the percentage of employed Negro males in the four occupational groups comprising the black bourgeoisie. In Table I, 16.3 per cent of the employed Negro males in the United States are in these occupations. In Table II we find that 16.3 per cent of the top incomes begin at the middle of the $2,000-$2,499 income bracket. For the South, 12.4 per cent of the top incomes begin at the bottom of this same income bracket. On the other hand, in the North and West where 24 per cent of the employed Negro males are in these occupations, 24 per cent of the top incomes begin with the $2,500-$2,999 income bracket.

12. C. Wright Mills, *White Collar* (New York: Oxford University Press, 1951), pp. 72-73.

13. Carter G. Woodson, *The Negro Professional Man and the Community* (Washington, D. C.: The Association for the Study of Negro Life and History, 1934), pp. 110-111, 175.

14. St. Clair Drake and Horace R. Cayton, *Black Metropolis*, pp. 478-84.

15. Joseph A. Pierce, *Negro Business and Business Education* (New York: Harper, 1947), p. vii.

16. *Ibid.*, p. 5. The criterion quoted is that the upper limits of small businesses are 250 workers employed, $250,000 as the value of assets, $100,000 net value or $1,000,000 in business volume.

17. W. E. B. DuBois, *The Negro in Business* (Atlanta: Atlanta University, 1898), p. 19.

18. Pierce, *op. cit.*, p. 69.

19. *Ibid.*, p. 35.

20. Drake and Cayton, *op. cit.*, p. 438.

21. Frazier, *The Negro in the United States*, pp. 406-407.

22. See U. S. Department of Commerce, *Business Information Service* (Washington, D. C., November, 1951).

23. Pierce, *op. cit.*, p. 100.

24. United States Department of Commerce, *Savings and Loan Associations Owned and Operated by Negroes* (Washington, D. C., 1951).

25. See Pierce, *op. cit.*, Chapter 6.

26. Vishnu V. Oak, *The Negro Newspaper* (Yellow Springs, Ohio: Antioch Press, 1948), pp. 66 ff.

27. The four leading newspapers had audited circulations in 1947 as follows: *Pittsburgh Courier* (all editions) 277,900; *Afro-American* (all editions) 235,600; *Chicago Defender* (both editions) 193,000; *Amsterdam News* (weekly total) 105,300. In 1947 the first three newspapers and the *Journal and Guide*, which are nationally circulating weeklies, had a total circulation of 750,000. See Oak, *op. cit.*, pp. 31, 70.

28. Oak, *op. cit.*, p. 72.

29. Pierce, *op. cit.*, pp. 112 ff.

## Chapter III

## Education of the Black Bourgeoisie

1. See Edward L. Pierce, "The Contrabands at Fortress Monroe," *Atlantic Monthly*, VIII (Nov. 1861), 626-40.

2. After General Butler applied the term "contraband" to these escaped slaves, the term was applied generally, first to Negroes who had been used by Confederates for military purposes, and later to all slaves of disloyal owners. See Bell Irwin Wiley, *Southern Negroes, 1861-1865* (New Haven: Yale University Press, 1938), pp. 176-77.

3. See Elizabeth Botume, *First Days Among the Contrabands* (Boston: Lee and Shepard, 1893), p. 79.

4. Horace Mann Bond, *The Education of the Negro in the American Social Order* (New York: Prentice-Hall, Inc., 1934), pp. 22-23.

5. *Ibid.*, p. 29.

6. See Frazier, *The Negro in the United States,* pp. 451-52.

7. Bond, *op. cit.*, pp. 131-33.

8. Dwight O. W. Holmes, *The Evolution of the Negro College* (New York: Columbia University Press, 1934), p. 165.

9. *Ibid.*, pp. 172 ff.

10. Frazier, *op. cit.*, p. 429.

11. *Selected Speeches of Booker T. Washington,* edited by E. Davidson Washington (New York: Doubleday, 1932), p. 34.

12. Booker T. Washington, who had no real university education and seemingly possessed little understanding of the changes which were occurring in the economic life of the United States, was simply proposing a program for teaching Negroes industrial skills which belonged to a handicraft stage of production. Moreover, he was seeking a means to enable Negroes to acquire industrial skills when the poor whites were supplanting Negroes as skilled artisans and were preventing them from acquiring mechanical skills by excluding them from apprenticeship and the emerging craft unions. See Sterling D. Spero and Abram L. Harris, *The Black Worker* (New York: Columbia University Press, 1931), pp. 16 ff., 48 ff. Washington's ideas were, of course, pedagogically sound when he insisted that education should be related to action and not purely verbal instruction unrelated to the experiences of the Negro. But he often exaggerated the defects of so-called "higher" education and minimized the role of intellectual discipline in education. Therefore, it was easy for southern whites to use his common-sense approach to the problems of Negro education to support their racial prejudice and for political purposes.

13. See *The Negro Problem. A Series of Articles by Representative Negroes of Today* (New York: James Potts and Co., 1903), pp. 60-61.

14. *Ibid.*, p. 33.

15. Evidence of this will be given in Chapter VI. Here it is relevant, however, to relate that when the writer taught at Tuskegee Institute in 1916-1917, he was told by the Director of the Academic Department to stop walking across the campus with books under his arms because white people passed through the campus and would get the impression that Tuskegee Institute was training the Negro's intellect rather than his heart and hand.

16. *Black-Belt Diamonds. Gems from the Speeches, Addresses, and Talks to Students of Booker T. Washington* (New York, Fortune and Scott), pp. 13-14.

17. Charles S. Johnson, *The Negro College Graduate* (Chapel Hill: University of North Carolina Press: 1938), Table LIV, p. 97.

18. *Black-Belt Diamonds*, pp. 20-21.

19. Leo Markun, *Mrs. Grundy. A History of Four Centuries of Morals in Great Britain and the United States Intended to Illuminate Present Problems* (New York: D. Appleton and Co., 1930), p. 506.

20. *Black-Belt Diamonds*, pp. 16-17.

21. *Ibid.*, pp. 39-40.

22. G. Raffalovich, "Piety Rules a Negro College," *Outlook*, 160

(Jan. 13, 1932) 45-46. In regard to the experience of this French professor, a number of observations should be made. When he began to teach at this Negro college a new generation of white northern missionaries had come into the South. Very often they were inferior to the missionaries who had gone South following the Civil War. The new generation of missionaries often accepted appointments in Negro schools because they could not secure employment in the North. Moreover, the missionary type of education for Negroes had become an anachronism after the first World War. The college in which he taught was one of the last strongholds of the missionary type of education. When these colleges were established by the missionaries, they provided a type of education for Negro students very similar to that provided for white students in the North.

23. *Selected Speeches of Booker T. Washington*, pp. 32-33.
24. *Black-Belt Diamonds*, pp. 91-92.
25. *Ibid.*, p. 14.
26. *Ibid.*, pp. 40-41.
27. *Ibid.*, p. 25.
28. *Ibid.*, p. 86.
29. See, for example, the case of Avery Normal Institute, which was founded by the American Missionary Association in 1866 in Charleston, South Carolina. In the Twentieth Annual Report is found the following statement:

What offered the greatest attraction to our best colored society is the fact that the Normal School is the recherché seminary, to which all the aristocracy send their children. This school is supported by the American Missionary Association of New York. The Rev. F. L. Cardoza is the principal. About three-fourths of the scholars are Freedmen, the remaining fourth (comprising the more advanced classes) being composed mostly of those who were born free, and who now constitute an aristocracy of color. . . . It is the design to make this a Normal School for the education of teachers, and the best material only has therefore been retained. . . . Although the greatest number of scholars in the more advanced classes are very fair, all hues are represented from the pale-faced Caucasian to the shining ebony of the native of Dahomey. (Quoted in Fred L. Brownlee, *New Day Ascending* [Boston: Pilgrim Press, 1946], pp. 135-36.)

30. See Bond, *op. cit.*, p. 362.
31. See Frazier, *The Negro in the United States*, pp. 471-73.

For the present situation in South Carolina, see the excellent study by Lewis K. McMillan, *Negro Higher Education in the State of South Carolina* (Orangeburg, South Carolina: the Author, 1952).

32. *Ibid.*, pp. 467 ff.

33. *Ibid.*, pp. 467-77.

34. The college described above by the French professor maintained a white administration until 1953.

35. See Ambrose Caliver, *A Background Study of Negro College Students* (Washington, D. C.: U. S. Government Printing Office, 1933), and by the same author, *A Personal Study of Negro College Students* (New York: Teachers College, Columbia University, 1931).

36. See U. S. Office of Education, *National Survey of the Higher Education of Negroes* (Washington, D. C.: 1942), II, pp. 42-43.

37. A Former Faculty Wife, "A Note on Intergroup Conditioning and Conflict Among an Interracial Faculty at a Negro College," *Social Forces*, XXVII (1949), 430-33.

38. Johnson, *op. cit.*, p. 92 ff.

39. Pierce, *Negro Business and Business Education*, pp. 239 ff.

40. *Ibid.*, p. 268.

# Chapter IV

# Power and Political Orientation

1. See *The Negro in the United States*, pp. 14-19, 335-343.

2. *Ibid.*, pp. 343 ff.

3. George F. Bragg, *History of the Afro-American Group of the Episcopal Church* (Baltimore: Church Advocate Press, 1922), p. 39.

4. Carter G. Woodson, *The History of the Negro Church* (2nd ed.; Washington: Associated Publishers, 1921), pp. 12 ff.

5. U. S. Bureau of the Census, *Statistical Abstract of the United States: 1952* (Washington, D. C., 1952), pp. 55-56.

6. See Horace A. White, "Who Owns the Negro Churches?" *Christian Century*, LV (1938), 176-177.

7. See Harold Van Buren Voorhis, P.M., *Negro Masonry in the United States* (New York: Emerson, 1940), pp. 3-22.

8. See Charles H. Brooks, *A History and Manual of the Grand United Order of Odd Fellows in America* (Philadelphia: M. V. P., Charles H. Brooks, 1893), pp. 19-20.

9. See *Why You Should Become a Knight and Daughter of Tabor*, p. 13 (pamphlet in the Mooreland Foundation, Howard

University, Washington, D. C.); W. P. Burrell and D. E. Johnson, *Twenty-five Years History of the Grand Fountain of the United Order of True Reformers* (Richmond, 1909), p. 12; Howard H. Turner, *Turner's History of the Independent Order of Good Samaritans and Daughters of Samaria,* Washington, 1881), pp. 25-26; and E. A. Williams, *History and Manual of the Colored Knights of Pythias* (Nashville: National Baptist Publishing Board, 1917), pp. 13-15.

10. See Harold F. Gosnell, *Negro Politicians* (Chicago: University of Chicago Press, 1935), pp. 68, 70, 110-111.

11. This statement is based upon the reports of persons connected with these organizations since there are no available statistics on the membership of the Negro secret societies. One estimate by Charles W. Ferguson in *Fifty Million Brothers* (New York: Farrar and Rinehart, Inc., 1937), p. 184, gave the membership as 2,500,000 with the property owned valued at $20,-000,000.

12. Ferguson, *op. cit.,* pp. 192-93.

13. See *Boulé Journal,* XIII (1946), for the history of the society.

14. See Charles H. Wesley, *The History of the Alpha Phi Alpha* (Washington, D. C.: Foundation Publishers, 1935), pp. 21-22.

15. See *The Negro in the United States,* pp. 383-385.

16. See Bond, *The Education of the Negro in the American Social Order,* pp. 53-56.

17. See L. Hollingworth Wood, "The Urban League Movement," *Journal of Negro History,* IX, pp. 117-126.

18. Horace R. Cayton and George S. Mitchell, *Black Workers and the New Unions* (Chapel Hill: University of North Carolina Press, 1939), p. 400.

19. *Ibid.,* p. 401.

20. See Cayton and Mitchell, *ibid.,* pp. 404 ff.; and Spero and Harris, *The Black Worker,* pp. 140-142.

21. See Spero and Harris, *op. cit.,* 141-142.

22. Cayton and Mitchell, *op. cit.,* 409-410.

23. See Myrdal, *op. cit.,* II, footnote, p. 841.

24. See Mary White Ovington, "The National Association for the Advancement of Colored People," *Journal of Negro History,* IX (1924), 107-116, and Robert L. Jack, *History of the National Association for the Advancement of Colored People* (Boston: Meador Publishing Co., 1943).

25. Ovington, *op. cit.,* p. 111.

26. See Spero and Harris, *op. cit.,* pp. 144-145.

27. Cayton and Mitchell, *op. cit.*, 414-415.

28. Since the Democratic Party was the only political party of any consequence in the South, the primary elections held for the nomination of the Party candidate really amounted to the election for office. When the election was subsequently held, only an insignificant number of Republican votes were cast.

29. See President's Committee on Fair Employment Practices, *Minorities in Defense* (Washington, 1941), and Myrdal, *op. cit.*, II, pp. 851-852.

30. V. O. Key, *Southern Politics* (New York: Knopf, 1949), pp. 286-291.

31. See Drake and Cayton, *op. cit.*, pp. 348 ff.; and Gosnell, *op. cit.*, pp. 24 ff.

32. See Gosnell, *op. cit.*, Chapter XV.

33. See Elmer W. Henderson, "Political Changes Among Negroes in Chicago During the Depression," *Social Forces*, XIX (May, 1941), 538-546. See also Drake and Cayton, *op. cit.*, pp. 353 ff.

34. See Gosnell, *op. cit.*, pp. 125 ff., concerning Negro political leaders who have been associated with the underworld.

35. One Negro political leader, who has many "business" operations in a northern city, said that he used to pay the Negro voters to vote against Roosevelt and the New Deal, but they were so *untrustworthy* that when alone in the voting booths they voted for Roosevelt. Therefore, he adopted the policy of paying them to refrain from voting.

36. It has been necessary to conceal the identity of this city as well as that of the Negro college in order to protect all persons concerned in this situation.

## Chapter V

## Break with the Traditional Background

1. See E. Franklin Frazier, *The Negro Family in the United States* (Chicago: University of Chicago Press, 1939), Chapter X, "The Sons of the Free."

2. *Ibid.*, pp. 391 ff.

3. See Lorenzo D. Turner, *Africanisms in the Gullah Dialect* (Chicago: University of Chicago Press, 1949).

4. See *The Negro Family in the United States*. Part I. "In the House of the Master."

5. See Newbell N. Puckett, *Folk Beliefs of the Southern Negro* (Chapel Hill: University of North Carolina Press).

6. See Melville J. Herskovits, *Life in a Haitian Valley* (New York: Knopf, 1937), and George E. Simpson, "Haitian Peasant Economy," *Journal of Negro History*, XXV (1940), 498-519.

7. See Roland Hayes, *My Songs, Aframerican Religious Folk Songs Arranged and Interpreted* (Boston: Little, Brown & Co., 1948).

8. See Sterling A. Brown, "The Blues as Folk Poetry," in B. A. Botkin, ed., *Folk Say. A Regional Miscellany* (Norman, Okla.: University of Oklahoma Press, 1930), pp. 324-39.

9. See Arthur A. Fausett, *Black Gods of the Metropolis* (Philadelphia: University of Pennsylvania Press, 1944).

10. See W. E. B. DuBois, "Marcus Garvey," *Crisis* (December, 1920 and January, 1921).

11. See Amy Jaques-Garvey, ed., *Philosophy and Opinions of Marcus Garvey* (New York: 1923), and T. G. Standing, "Nationalism in Negro Leadership," *American Journal of Sociology*, XL, pp. 180-192.

12. See E. Franklin Frazier, "Garvey: A Mass Leader," *Nation*, CXIII (August, 1926), 147-48.

13. E. Franklin Frazier, "The Garvey Movement," *Opportunity*, IV (1926), 346-48.

14. One prosperous American Negro doctor in Chicago remarked to the writer that Garvey's U.N.I.A. (Universal Negro Improvement Association) really stood for the Ugliest Negroes in America.

15. See *The New Negro,* ed. Alain Locke (New York: Albert and Charles Boni, 1925), pp. 4, 8. Locke offers a purely idealistic explanation of the changes in the relation of Negroes to American society. According to him, "Neither Labor demands, the boll-weevil nor the Ku Klux Klan is a basic factor, however contributory any or all of them may have been. The wash and rush of this human tide on the beach line of northern city centers is to be explained primarily in terms of a new vision of opportunity, of social and economic freedom, of a spirit to seize, even in the face of an extortionate and heavy toll, a change for the improvement of condition." (*Op. cit.,* p. 6).

16. Sterling A. Brown, *Negro Poetry and Drama* (Washington, D. C.: Associates in Negro Folk Education, 1937), p. 61.

17. See Sterling Brown, *Southern Road* (New York: Harcourt, 1932).

18. See Robert E. Park, "Negro Consciousness as Reflected in Race Literature," *American Review*, I, pp. 509-17.

19. Frazier, "Durham: Capital of the Black Middle Class," in

Locke, ed., *The New Negro,* pp. 333-40.

20. Georges Friedmann, *Où va le travail humain* (Paris: Gallimard, 1950).

21. See Drake and Cayton, *Black Metropolis,* Chapter 19. The old upper class, like the new upper class, in the Negro community was composed of middle-class Negroes whose position in the Negro community caused them to play the role of an upper class.

22. *Ibid.,* pp. 546-550.

## Chapter VI

## Inferiority Complex and Quest for Status

1. See William MacDonald, *Documentary Source Book of American History* (New York: Macmillan, 1914), p. 218.

2. See Frederick Bancroft, *Slave-Trading in the Old South* (Baltimore: J. H. Furst Co., 1931), p. 365.

3. See Carl Becker, *The Declaration of Independence* (New York: Knopf, 1942), p. 212.

4. W. E. B. DuBois, *Suppression of the African Slave-Trade* (New York: Longmans, 1896), pp. 123-124, 178-187.

5. See Ellen Hellman, *Rooiyard: A Sociological Survey of an Urban Native Slum Yard* (Capetown: Oxford University Press, 1948), p. 110, where she defines detribalization according to three criteria: "permanent residence in an area other than that of the chief to whom a man would normally pay allegiance; complete severance of relationship to the chief; and independence of rural relatives both for support during periods of unemployment and ill-health or for the performances of ceremonies connected with the major crises of life."

6. See C. F. Pascoe, *Two Hundred Years of the S.P.G.: An Historical Account of the Society for the Propagation of the Gospel in Foreign Parts* (London: 1901), I, pp. 1-13.

7. W. E. B. DuBois, *The Negro Church* (Atlanta: Atlanta University Press, 1903), p. 21.

8. George D. Armstrong, *The Christian Doctrine of Slavery* (New York: C. Scribner, 1851), p. 134.

9. Rev. Fred. A. Ross, *Slavery Ordained of God* (Philadelphia: Lippincott, 1857), p. 5.

10. See "Professor Thomas R. Dew on Slavery," in *The Proslavery Argument* (Philadelphia: 1853), pp. 287-490.

11. Frances A. Kemble, *Journal of a Residence on a Georgian Plantation in 1838-1839* (New York: Harper, 1863), pp. 193-194.

12. *Ibid.,* p. 194.

13. See *Negro Population, 1790-1915,* p. 208.

14. See *The Negro Family in the United States,* pp. 65-85.

15. E. Horace Fitchett, "The Traditions of the Free Negroes of Charleston, South Carolina," *Journal of Negro History,* XXV (1940), 139-152.

16. MacDonald, *Documentary Source Book of American History, 1608-1898,* pp. 405-420.

17. Mervin Roe, ed., *Speeches and Letters of Abraham Lincoln, 1832-1865* (New York: Dutton, 1907), p. 194.

18. *Ibid.,* p. 195.

19. Charles A. Beard and Mary R. Beard, *The Rise of American Civilization* (New York, 1927) II, pp. 81-84.

20. DuBois, *Black Reconstruction,* p. 56.

21. Bell, I. Wiley, *Southern Negroes, 1861-1865* (New Haven: Yale University Press, 1938), pp. 303-310.

22. DuBois, *op. cit.,* p. 97.

23. Carl R. Fish, *The Rise of the Common Man* (New York: Macmillan, 1927), pp. 280 ff.

24. See Thomas W. Higginson, *Army Life in a Black Regiment* (Boston: Fields, Osgood, 1870).

25. See *The Negro in the United States,* pp. 126-128.

26. See Louis M. Hacker, *The Triumph of American Capitalism* (New York: Simon and Schuster, 1940), pp. 378-379, and C. Vann Woodward, *Reunion and Reaction. The Compromise of 1877 and the End of Reconstruction* (Boston: Little, Brown, 1951).

27. See Rayford W. Logan, *The Negro in American Life and Thought: The Nadir, 1877-1901* (New York: Dial Press, 1925).

28. See Arthur F. Raper, *The Tragedy of Lynching* (Chapel Hill: University of North Carolina Press, 1933), p. 480.

29. See *The Negro in the United States,* pp. 160-161.

30. Quoted in Paul Lewison, *Race, Class and Party* (New York: Oxford University Press, 1932), pp. 84-85.

31. See William A. Sinclair, *The Aftermath of Slavery* (Boston: Small, Maynard, 1905), p. 105. This book contains an excellent account of the methods which were used to reduce the Negro to a subordinate caste in the South.

32. Quoted in Logan, *op. cit.,* p. 90. This book provides the only comprehensive study and thorough documentation on the position of the Negro in American society during this period.

33. Chas. Carroll, *The Negro a Beast* (St. Louis: American Book and Bible House, 1900).

34. *Ibid.,* p. 339.

35. Howard W. Odum, *Social and Mental Traits of the Negro*

(New York: Columbia University, 1910), p. 171. Dr. Odum who, as head of the Department of Sociology of the University of North Carolina has done much to encourage scientific studies of the Negro, has long ago learned better than to accept any such notions concerning the Negro. Nevertheless, his book was very influential at the time in giving "scientific" support to prejudiced opinion concerning the Negro in the United States.

36. See Charles H. McCord, *The American Negro as a Dependent, Defective, and Delinquent* (Nashville: Benson Printing Co., 1914), p. 42.

37. R. W. Shuffeldt, M. D., *America's Greatest Problem: The Negro* (Philadelphia: F. A. Davis, 1915), p. 47.

38. See Mary White Ovington, *Half a Man* (New York: Longmans, 1911).

39. In 1908, Charles Francis Adams of the famous Adams family, influential in the history of the United States since the American Revolution, declared that the American theory concerning the assimilation of all races had broken in regard to the Negro since he was "a foreign substance" that could "neither be assimilated nor thrown out." Quoted in Robert E. Park and Ernest W. Burgess, *Introduction to the Science of Sociology* (Chicago: University of Chicago Press, 1924), p. 760.

40. See Edward B. Reuter, *The Mulatto in the United States* (Boston: Richard G. Badger, Gorham Press, 1918) for a study of the extent of race mixture and the role of the mixed-bloods among Negroes in the United States. This book is the most important source of information on the mulatto or Negro of mixed ancestry up to the second decade of the present century, despite the fact that it reflects some of the current prejudices of whites and contains a number of serious errors. For example, the author states on p. 317 that "In the United States almost every Negro of prominence from Frederick Douglass to Jack Johnson has married a white woman or a light-colored mulatto." While it was very likely true that the majority of prominent Negroes, who were themselves mulattoes, married mulattoes, only a negligible number of prominent Negroes married white women.

41. W. E. Burghardt DuBois, *The Souls of Black Folks* (15th ed.; Chicago, 1926), p. 109.

# Chapter VII
# Negro Business: A Social Myth

1. Abram L. Harris, *The Negro as Capitalist*, pp. 49-50.
2. Quoted in *Ibid.*, pp. 51-52.

3. Quoted in *Ibid.*, p. 53.

4. *Proceedings of the National Negro Business League*. First meeting held in Boston, Massachusetts, August 23 and 24, 1900. (Copyright 1901).

5. *Ibid.*, p. 26.

6. *Ibid.*, p. 129.

7. *Ibid.*, p. 259.

8. *Ibid.*, p. 200.

9. *The Negro in Business*, ed. W. E. B. Dubois (Atlanta: Atlanta University Press, 1899), p. 50.

10. Booker T. Washington, *The Negro in Business* (Boston: Hertel, 1907), p. 275.

11. *Ibid.*

12. *Ibid.*, p. 136.

13. *Report of the Eleventh Annual Convention of the National Negro Business League* (Nashville: A. M. E. Sunday School Union, 1911), p. 11.

14. *Ibid.*, pp. 78-85.

15. *Ibid.*, p. 81.

16. *Ibid.*, p. 83.

17. See Pierce, *Negro Business and Business Education*, p. 152.

18. *Report of the Thirteenth Annual Convention of the National Negro Business League* (Washington, D. C., n.d.), p. 52.

19. *Report of the Fifteenth Annual Convention of the National Negro Business League* (Washington, D. C., n.d.), pp. 83-84.

20. Albion L. Holsey, *Booker T. Washington's Own Story of His Life and Work* (Washington, D. C., 1915), pp. 407-409.

21. *National Negro Business League* (Washington, D. C., n.d.), p. 124.

22. Pierce, *op. cit.*, pp. 210-211.

23. Quoted in *Annual Report of the Secretary's Office, National Negro Business League, for the fiscal year ending August 15, 1929*, p. 2.

24. Pierce, *op. cit.*, p. 211. See also Harris, *The Negro as Capitalist*, p. 178.

25. See Pierce, *op. cit.*, "Book Two," concerning the development and character of business education in Negro colleges.

26. Pierce, *op. cit.*, p. 277.

27. *The Post-War Outlook for Negroes in Small Business, The Engineering Professions, and Technical Vocations* (Papers and Proceedings of the Ninth Annual Conference of the Division of the Social Sciences, Howard University, Washington, D. C., 1946), p. 29.

28. Pierce, *op. cit.*, p. vi.

29. See Drake and Cayton, *op. cit.*, pp. 430-432.

30. Harris, *op. cit.*, pp. 182-184.

31. See *The Post-War Outlook for Negroes*.

32. *Ibid.*, pp. 8-9.

33. See *Program of the Fiftieth Anniversary. National Negro Business League.* Tuskegee, Alabama, August 29-September 1, 1950.

34. *Ibid.*, p. 3.

35. Without any basis in available statistics on the purchasing power of Negroes, an advertising magazine, *Tide*, July 20, 1951, made the statement that Negroes were spending $15 billion in 1951. This same unfounded statement was repeated in an article entitled "The Negro—Progress and Challenge," in the *New York Times Magazine*, February 7, 1954, by Chester Bowles. Although I wrote a letter to the *New York Times* showing that, on the basis of available statistics, Negroes could not have spent more than $6 billion in 1951, the letter was never published.

36. After the writer had used the term "lumpen-bourgeoisie" to describe the black bourgeoisie, he discovered that C. Wright Mills in his *White Collar* (New York: University Press, 1951, pp. 28-33) had used this term to designate the multitude of white firms "with a high death rate, which do a fraction of the total business done in their lines and engage a considerably larger proportion of people than their quota of business."

## Chapter VIII

## The Negro Press and Wish-Fulfillment

1. See Frederick G. Detweiler, *The Negro Press in the United States* (Chicago: University of Chicago Press, 1922), pp. 35-36.

2. *Ibid.*, pp. 53 ff.

3. See "Documents: Letters of Negro Migrants of 1916-1918," *Journal of Negro History*, IV (1919), 290-340; and "Additional Letters of Negro Migrants of 1916-1918," *ibid.*, IV (1919), 412-465.

4. Frazier, *The Negro in the United States*, p. 504.

5. According to the United States Department of Commerce, "Negro Newspapers and Periodicals in the United States, 1943," *Negro Statistical Bulletin*, No. 1 (August, 1944), 67.4 per cent of the 144 Negro newspapers reporting year of establishment were less than 25 years old.

6. Myrdal, *An American Dilemma*, pp. 908-912.

7. See *Pittsburgh Courier. Washington Edition*, May 22, 1954, p. 12.

8. *Ibid.*, p. 12.

9. *Ibid.*, May 1, 1954, p. 12.

10. *Ibid.*, May 22, 1954, p. 12.

11. *Ibid.*, May 8, 1954, p. 12.

12. *Ibid.*, April 3, 1954. See *Afro-American. Magazine Section*, April 18, 1950.

13. *Ebony*, IV (April, 1949).

14. *Ibid.*, August, 1949.

15. See Washington *Afro-American*, June 8, 1954.

16. See *Pittsburgh Courier. Washington Edition*, March 20, 1954.

17. See *Pittsburgh Courier. Washington Edition*, May 15, 1954.

18. See (Norfolk) *Journal and Guide*, June 5, 1954.

19. See front page feature article entitled "Black Troops Were There," in the *Pittsburgh Courier. Washington Edition*, May 15, 1954.

20. *Ebony*, September, 1954

## Chapter IX

## "Society": Status without Substance

1. Austin Steward, *Twenty-two Years a Slave, and Forty Years a Freeman* (Rochester. Allings and Cory, 1857), pp. 30-32.

2. Manuscript document by John E. Bruce in the Schomburg Collection, New York.

3. It is difficult to find a file of *The Washington Bee*, which published these attacks on the mulattoes.

4. See Drake and Cayton, *op. cit.*, pp. 470 ff.

5. See *Jet*, December 27, 1951.

6. See, for example, pictures of Dr. Bunche being presented with the diamond cross of Malta in *The Philadelphia Tribune*, January 2, 1951.

7. See *The Pittsburgh Courier. Washington Edition*, January 10, 1953.

8. Compare Myrdal, *op. cit.*, pp. 918-919, 952-55.

9. Once I was asked to write a criticism of an article which a Negro had written in a scientific journal. The dean of a Negro college, who read the article and my criticism, objected to what I wrote on the grounds that I had treated the article in the scientific journal seriously!

10. See *Jet*, August 12, 1954, p. 6. Italics mine.

11. Cited in Myrdal, *op. cit.*, p. 919.

12. Mary H. Kingsley, *Travels in West Africa, Congo Français, Corisco and Cameroons.* (London: Macmillan, 1897), pp. 660-61.

# Chapter X
## Behind the Masks

1. E. Franklin Frazier, *Negro Youth at the Crossways* (Washington, D. C.: American Council on Education, 1940), p. 62.

2. *Ibid.*, p. 67.

3. *Ibid.*, p. 66.

4. See, for example, the article "YMCA Secretary in Virginia Fired for Equality Fight," *Washington Afro-American,* August, 1954, p. 20.

5. One can not determine to what extent homosexuality among Negro males is due to the fact that they can not play a "masculine role."

6. See *Ebony*, July, 1949, where it is claimed that a poll on the most exciting Negro men in the United States reveals that the heyday of the "glamour boy" is gone and achievement rather than a handsome face and husky physique is the chief factor in making Negro men exciting to women.

7. See Robert E. Park and Ernest W. Burgess, *Introduction to the Science of Sociology* (Chicago: University of Chicago Press, 1924), p. 139.

8. See Kardiner and Ovesey, *op. cit.*, pp. 312 ff. concerning this point.

9. See Frazier, *The Negro Family in the United States*, pp. 440-43.

10. Robert E. Park, "Negro Home Life and Standards of Living," in *The Negro's Progress in Fifty Years* (Philadelphia: American Academy of Political and Social Science, 1913), p. 163.

11. See Charles S. Johnson, *Patterns of Negro Segregation* (New York: Harper, 1943), Chapters XII, XIII, and XIV which describe the ways in which Negroes in various classes deal with racial discrimination.

12. See Kardiner and Ovesey, *op. cit.*, pp. 190, 282, 297.

13. *Ibid.*, p. 177.

14. *Ibid.*, p. 203.

15. *Ibid.*, pp. 313 ff.

# Conclusion

1. *The Autobiography of Alice B. Toklas* (New York: Harcourt, Brace, 1933), p. 292.

# Index